T0302039

A LEADERSHIP JOURNEY IN HEALTH CARE

Virginia Mason's Story

leadership throughout the organization. Every company can learn from VM's leadership examples. A must read if you are interested in unlocking the hidden value within your company."

Art Byrne
Former CEO of The Wiremold Company and
author of The Lean Turnaround

"This practical leadership guide shares the strategy, the management tools and systems, and a vision of the culture needed to thrive in today's challenging health care world. Readers will get a detailed view of the Virginia Mason Production System and the methods that Virginia Mason leaders use to achieve world-class results for their patients."

Maureen Bisognano
President and CEO, Institute for Healthcare Improvement

"Talented people leading and working together on a comprehensive continuous improvement strategy and relentless implementation plan to deliver a compelling vision! Virginia Mason's Story has important lessons for all of us!!"

Alan Mulally
Retired CEO of Ford and Boeing Commercial Airplanes

A LEADERSHIP JOURNEY IN HEALTH CARE

Virginia Mason's Story

Charles Kenney

FOREWORD BY CAROLYN CORVI

*Virginia Mason Health System/Virginia Mason Medical Center
Boards of Directors; Retired Vice President and
General Manager Boeing Commercial Airplanes.
Boeing Lean management leader*

CRC Press
Taylor & Francis Group
Boca Raton London New York

CRC Press is an imprint of the
Taylor & Francis Group, an **informa** business
A PRODUCTIVITY PRESS BOOK

CRC Press
Taylor & Francis Group
6000 Broken Sound Parkway NW, Suite 300
Boca Raton, FL 33487-2742

First issued in paperback 2021

© 2015 by Virginia Mason Medical Center
CRC Press is an imprint of Taylor & Francis Group, an Informa business

No claim to original U.S. Government works

ISBN 13: 978-1-03-209855-5 (pbk)
ISBN 13: 978-1-4822-9968-7 (hbk)

Visit the Taylor & Francis Web site at
http://www.taylorandfrancis.com

and the CRC Press Web site at
http://www.crcpress.com

Contents

Foreword

"If Lean management generates the improvements its apostles advertise, then why don't more companies adopt and sustain it as their management method?"

Through the years, I have been asked this question many times. As a student of the Toyota Production System principles and practices for more than two decades, I am still puzzled by why more organizations either don't adopt this Lean management method or for those that do, why they are unable to sustain it. There is no question that the Toyota method works—I have witnessed its transformative power, improving quality, safety and efficiency in industries ranging from aircraft manufacturing to health care.

Over time, I have come to believe that the answer to the question above has everything to do with people; more precisely, the failure by many companies to truly understand that "respect for people" lies at the heart of the management method. This may seem surprising when we think about a system that may initially appear mechanistic. It is true that Lean management has many technical aspects based on improvement science—measurement, standardization, and the disciplined application of a particular set of tools. But my experience is that underneath it all—beneath the metrics, the standard work, the kaizen events—lies a management method with a beating heart; a steady rhythm that tightly links the method to the human beings who apply it. Organizations that succeed in sustaining the Toyota method—Virginia Mason included—possess a visceral understanding of the essential role "respect for people" plays in keeping this management method alive and sustainable.

"Respect for people" is just one of the attributes that have enabled Virginia Mason to progress. In this book you will read stories that clearly describe the impact the Virginia Mason Production System has had (the adaptation of the Toyota Production System to health care) in keeping patients safe; in providing some of the highest quality care anywhere; and in improving both access and affordability. The book contains engaging stories about particular improvement initiatives and stories about impactful leadership at all levels of the organization. What makes this book both different and particularly insightful is that it gets at Virginia Mason's beating heart. It reveals that a deep sense of humanity, a deep "respect for people" is embedded in the organization's DNA. Virginia Mason is a mission driven organization where intrinsic motivation is woven throughout the culture. We are guided by Paul O'Neill's dictum that great organizations are ones where employees answer yes to these three questions:

- Can I say every day I am treated with dignity and respect by everyone I encounter without respect to my pay grade, or my title, or my race, or ethnicity or religious beliefs or gender?
- Am I given the things I need—education, training, tools, and encouragement—to develop my full potential so I can make a contribution to the organization that gives meaning to my life?
- Am I recognized and appreciated for the work I do?

The focus in our contemporary business culture for instant gratification—the curse of short term thinking—is both aligned with and contrary to the Toyota methods. In the short run, Lean techniques enable major leaps, yet sustaining progress requires an eternal commitment. When managers think of Lean as a program or initiative, the battle is already lost. For an organization to continuously improve it must be a way of *being*. At Virginia Mason, we are able to sustain the work because the Toyota approach, founded on "respect for people", is not a program, or an initiative, or something we do in addition to our daily work. It is our daily work, and the foundation for everything we do.

With a belief in and "respect for people" (employees, patients and their families), dedication to continuous improvement, constancy of purpose and consistent leadership, we are positioned to forge ahead in our mission *to be the quality leader and transform health care*. It is a journey without end. Have we made progress? Certainly. But if you ask anyone here at Virginia Mason whether we can do better, they will tell you that we can do *much* better. The beauty of this management method in combination with the dedicated people at Virginia Mason who apply it, is that although we have not yet achieved the perfect patient experience, every day we inch a little bit closer.

Carolyn Corvi

(Carolyn Corvi has served on the Virginia Mason Health System/ Virginia Mason Medical Center Boards of Directors for 13 years, four as chair. She is the former vice president-general manager of Airplane Programs, Boeing Commercial Airplanes, and Boeing Lean management leader. She was responsible for leading Commercial Airplanes integrated production system—including design, production and delivery of the 737, 747, 767 and 777.)

A Leadership Story

What does leadership look like? Is it a courageous act by a charismatic individual? Is it heroic action? A caped crusader saving the day? Is it Justice Stewart's memorable definition of obscenity—*I know it when I see it?* Does leadership look like an iconic individual? Steve Jobs, for example? How about leadership in health care? Is it the image of a white-coated chief of medicine? A confident surgeon?

This book seeks to answer the question, "What does leadership look like?" with a particular focus on Virginia Mason Medical Center. I have written about Virginia Mason in several books and on the Virginia Mason blog (virginiamasonblog.org). One of the books, *Transforming Health Care: Virginia Mason Medical Center's Pursuit of the Perfect Patient Experience,* tells the story of pioneering work adapting the Toyota Production System to health care. Much of the health care world now knows about that lean work, about advances in safety, quality, access, and affordability. Much of the work is so good that the Virginia Mason Institute was formed to respond to the demand for teaching and coaching scores of health care organizations throughout the United States and beyond.

Until now, Virginia Mason has been recognized for its breakthrough work using the Virginia Mason Production System. But in recent years it has grown increasingly clear that there is much more to Virginia Mason than the Toyota method. It has become clear, in fact, that at its core the essential Virginia Mason narrative is really a story about leadership. Sometimes it is leadership in the form of a strong individual with the vision to see what needs to be done and the courage to implement it—however unpopular it may be in the moment.

Far more often than not, however, you see it in other forms; you see it not in a heroic act but in a *process* designed entirely around the needs of patients, in the *culture*, in standard work that is designed and followed by the teams at the front lines of care. As you make your way throughout the organization leadership is visible. You see it in a kaizen event, in standard work, in executive rounding.

These images of leadership lack the inherent drama of caped crusaders. They are the antithesis of the heroic Dr. Houses of the world, the Hugh Laurie television character whose individual intuition and genius invariably saved the day. Sarah Patterson, Virginia Mason chief operating officer, has a term for the House-like heroic action: *management by superheroes*. While highly entertaining on TV, Patterson notes that "it is a dangerous way to provide care because it is the opposite of the reliability and calm you need to provide great care every day. Leaders often get to where they are by being good crisis managers. But we believe that a crisis is really a failure of leadership."

Leadership at Virginia Mason can be seen when a management method is firmly in place; when an organization is aligned in its mission and goals; when supervisors teach, monitor, and coach at the front lines of care. Leadership is visible in core organizational attributes—optimism, accountability, courage, transparency, and more.

At Virginia Mason you can see leadership in how people treat one another, in disruptive governance changes that challenge longstanding traditions, in the absence of siloes. You see it embodied in the most audacious of goals: to transform health care, not just at Virginia Mason but across the world.

What has become ever clearer is that the approach to leadership at Virginia Mason has the potential to work in just about any health care organization—or in any enterprise for that matter, health care or otherwise—where there is inherent complexity.

This book seeks to provide a firsthand look inside of the walls of Virginia Mason—throughout the organization—where leadership is visible everywhere.

Chapter 1

To Be the Quality Leader and Transform Health Care

At the University of Texas Medical Branch in Galveston, Kathy Shingleton enjoyed perks afforded to many senior health care executives. On her first day of employment, she drove to work, bypassing all those employees who were looking for parking spots on the street or blocks from campus, and she pulled into a designated spot marked by her name and title. She walked a short distance to her corner office, filled with custom cherry furniture and upholstered chairs. Her view encompassed the Gulf of Mexico where, on many evenings, the sunsets were showstoppers.

When Kathy was recruited to be the vice president of human resources for Virginia Mason in 2011, she found herself in a very different situation. She was a highly qualified candidate for the position, with her MBA and PhD in education and leadership. She had served in a variety of successively more responsible positions at the University of Texas for 23 years. When Kathy arrived for work in Seattle, she discovered that parking was not available on campus because those slots were reserved for patients. She scrambled to find off-campus parking and ended up parking three blocks away and having to walk up a steep hill to arrive at her office. (To make matters worse, the parking she was able to locate required her to pick up her car by 6 pm every evening. So as a result, some evenings she would have to move her car to another parking lot.)

And then she arrived at the "executive suite" of offices. This involved descending a flight of concrete steps to the basement of a three-story structure built in the 1940s. She entered the bunker-like facility, which formerly served as a hospital warehouse and supply area. Her office—about one-fifth the size of her Galveston space—was nearly identical to the other 13 offices occupied by senior executives along the subterranean hallway: 12 by 12 foot spaces, low ceilings, small desk, and table, and of course no windows. "When they showed me to my office, I kind of laughed," recalls Kathy. "I thought, *'Okaaayyy.'* In Texas executives got parking spaces first, and then patients got what was left. When I came to Virginia Mason it was immediately clear that the patients came first in *everything.*"

Sometimes appearances matter. Sometimes something as mundane as a parking space offers clues to a richer story—a story that speaks of a deeper culture. The executives along Kathy's hallway reside there because space in any medical center is a precious commodity and the best available space at Virginia Mason goes to patients.

Consider the case of the renovated cancer center. When the facility was nearly completed, architects and designers met with staff members who would be working within the space: doctors, nurses, receptionists, medical assistants, and more. This was in the earliest days of the Virginia Mason adaptation of the Toyota Production System to health care—a time when the current culture was in its infancy. When the staff gathered in the new space several physicians laid claim to one office or another, spaces on the exterior of the floor with large windows and plentiful natural light. But then something happened that has been repeated over and over again every day many thousands of times since then. Someone in the room uttered the words that possess more power than anything else at Virginia Mason: *Who is at the top of our pyramid? Who comes first in everything we do?* And the team fell silent for a moment as people looked at one another. Suddenly there was clarity: *Of course* the perimeter rooms would go to patients! These perimeter spaces with natural light and leafy views became infusion rooms where cancer patients enjoyed reclining lounge chairs, flat-screen TVs, wireless Internet, and small refrigerators with cold drinks. And so it was that the physicians and other staff members occupied the inner portion of the floor, an arrangement enabling staff members to communicate easily and serve patients well.

Virginia Mason Is *Different*

Denise Dubuque experienced the difference firsthand when she left Virginia Mason in 2008 to take a position at another provider organization. "At Virginia Mason we had an egalitarian sense that every team member has something valuable to add," she says. "That is for real at Virginia Mason. It is real and it is in the DNA. It's not just words. And that's why I came back. I believe anything is possible at Virginia Mason. Sometimes the more urgently something needs to be done the better the work we do. We make things happen quickly. We are agile in responding to whatever is happening. And I think we are set up to be really successful in this crazy, turbulent health care environment."

Virginia Mason is different from other provider organizations throughout the nation in many ways, and the most obvious differentiator is the organization's success during the past dozen years in adapting the Toyota Production System as its management method. Virginia Mason is recognized as among the leaders—perhaps *the* leader—in applying *lean* management to health care. While that distinction lies at the core of what differentiates Virginia Mason from the vast majority of health care organizations in the United States, it is certainly not the only distinguishing characteristic.

Virginia Mason's declared vision, for example, is "to be the quality leader and transform health care." This does not mean the quality leader and transform health care in Seattle or the Northwest but *throughout the United States.* Jim Young, chair of the Virginia Mason board of directors, says that he, along with his board and management colleagues, wholeheartedly embraces this idea: "I do not believe it is overly audacious for us to want to transform health care across the country."

Carolyn Corvi, Virginia Mason board member and former executive vice president at Boeing where she led production of the enormously successful 737 line of aircraft, puts it this way:

> We are a place so many people come to learn. We can be a signpost for anybody who is serious about wanting to improve quality, safety, and affordability. The imperative in health care is to change and innovate fast—we owe it to every family in America to do that—to get much better much faster. We must transform nationally, balancing speed with the ability to make change sustainable. What concerns me is that people are wasting time grasping at different methods to try to do this. I am convinced, based on what we have accomplished at Virginia Mason, that there is no better way to do this. People shouldn't fumble around experimenting with different methods. They should recognize that this is the better way and get on with it.

Since Virginia Mason began applying Toyota Production System–inspired principles more than a decade ago, the organization has achieved significant advances in quality, safety, and efficiency, all while lowering costs. Virginia Mason's experience over more than a decade is living proof that the most effective affordability strategy is the relentless pursuit of quality. As of 2014, all major inpatient procedures and care episodes at Virginia Mason were 20–60 percent more affordable than they are at other Seattle-area hospitals and well below the national average. If Virginia Mason's results were somehow applied across the nation the quality, safety and cost challenges in American health care would be all but solved.

Since adapting the Toyota Production System to health care in 2001, Virginia Mason has achieved world-class levels of patient satisfaction across the organization and has been honored as one of the safest hospitals in the country—so safe that the cost of professional liability insurance at Virginia Mason has declined 74 percent since 2005. Throughout the financial crisis starting in 2008, there were no layoffs at Virginia Mason and the organization continued to share annual bonuses with employees. When Intel Corporation sought to improve the quality of care for their employees while controlling costs, they partnered with a team at

Virginia Mason. When Wal-Mart sought the highest quality and value for their employees, they selected a small handful of providers including Virginia Mason to deliver specialty care in cardiology, spine care, and total joint replacements.

Virginia Mason teams have reduced operating room turn times in some cases to just 22 minutes and have cut wait time for patients with low back pain from 31 days to same-day access. Women seeking mammograms park their cars and have completed the process in so little time there is no parking fee. Previously, nurses in the hospital spent only about 35–40 percent of their time with patients—now they spend 90 percent. During the past three years hospital stay for total knee replacement has been reduced from nearly 4 days in 2012 (the national average is 3.6 days), to 2.5 days in early 2013, to 36 hours for a subset of patients in late 2013. The instrument set up time for a craniotomy procedure has been reduced from 24 minutes to 2 minutes, 41 seconds. Virginia Mason was the first hospital in the world to require all staff to obtain flu vaccine as a fitness for duty requirement.

These and thousands of other improvements are the result of Virginia Mason's signature achievement: creating a new way of managing health care that works at every level. A measure of the effectiveness of Virginia Mason's approach is the demand from other health care organizations travelling to Seattle to learn—so much demand that Virginia Mason formed the Virginia Mason Institute to teach others. Since the formation of the institute in 2008, more than 4,000 physicians, administrators, and other health care professionals from 50 states and more than 20 nations throughout the world have made the trip to Seattle.

The question is why? Why have so many health care professionals traveled to the Northwest corner of the United States to learn how to do health care? The answer, according to Press Ganey, is that "Virginia Mason has become the learning lab of health care transformation. Its work has shown it is possible to achieve higher-quality and safer care while lowering costs, improving patient satisfaction, almost eliminating staff turnover and staying competitive business-wise" (September/October 2012).

Let's consider that statement for a moment. For several decades Press Ganey has been focused on identifying and measuring patient-focused quality in health care. The company works with more than 10,000 organizations globally and fully half of all hospitals in the United States. It is a notable achievement when an organization of this size and reach concludes that Virginia Mason is "the learning lab of health care transformation." When health care professionals travel to Seattle in search of knowledge, they invariably ask Virginia Mason teams: How did you *do* this? How have you progressed so far on quality, safety, access, efficiency, finances, and affordability?

The Characteristics that Differentiate Virginia Mason

We have noted that Virginia Mason is different from most other health care organizations in its adaption of the Toyota method and in its vision to transform health care. Digging a bit deeper we find other characteristics that differentiate the organization. Virginia Mason has a crystal clear vision of where it wants to go, alignment throughout the organization toward that goal, a management method and tools to reach the goal, and a culture of respect for people that enables strong teamwork and rapid innovation. The Virginia Mason Production System includes a number of critical elements:

A *Shared vision,* outlined within a Strategic Plan that places the patient first in everything, always.

Aligned expectations achieved through deep conversations known as compacts. Compacts exist for board members, leaders, and physicians clarifying their responsibilities to the organization and reciprocal obligations the organization has toward them.

A *single-improvement method*, with the tools and methods of lean enabling improvements in quality, safety, access, efficiency, and affordability every day at every level of the organization.

A *culture* predicated on deep respect for people and continuous improvement.

Visitors to Virginia Mason seek the secret formula, but of course it is no one thing. Rather, it is the synergistic power of these elements—shared vision, aligned expectations, the Virginia Mason Production System, and a culture of respect. Each one individually is central to the mission, but it is their collective power that fuels so many simultaneous improvements. It is clearly a case where the whole is an order of magnitude more powerful than the sum of the parts. All of this makes for a level of alignment rarely found in health care and that alignment centers on the patient. As Dr. Gary Kaplan, Virginia Mason chief executive officer, puts it: "Patient first is the heart of everything we do. Patient first is our most transformative element."

Alignment is among the most powerful forces in health care today, yet it seems as rare as it is powerful. At Virginia Mason there is alignment of mission and values from the board of directors through the executive leadership and throughout the entire organization. This alignment enables common focus, a common goal, a common language, and a common culture. When people come to visit they often find that everybody at Virginia Mason says the same thing. And that speaks to authentic alignment on goals, vision, and mission. "When you come here to Virginia Mason you do not see competing missions and goals from one group or department to another," says Sarah Patterson, COO. "You see an aligned organization. We all work on the entire body of work. *All* the executives are responsible for *all* the goals."

And one of those goals—the most important goal, in fact—is patient safety. Since the tragic death of a patient due to a preventable medical error Virginia Mason has become one of the safest medical centers anywhere. The death of Mrs. Mary McClinton in 2004 motivates Virginia Mason teams every day to push for safety improvements recognized throughout the world, so much so that when the leader of the National Health Service in Great Britain wanted to address safety improvements in his system he traveled to Seattle to announce his new program at Virginia Mason.

"Virginia Mason is one of the safest hospitals in the world and perhaps the safest in the world," said Jeremy Hunt, secretary of state for health in the United Kingdom. Hunt sought to address a scandal in which negligent care in the United Kingdom resulted in "suffering of hundreds of people"—including deaths at the Mid Staffordshire hospital trust in England.

What Does Leadership *Look* Like?

Central to the Virginia Mason story is the use of a management system that enables teams to eliminate waste while improving safety, access, quality, and affordability. Underneath all of that—underpinning *all* of the work that Virginia Mason has done during the past 14 years—is leadership: steady, committed, present, aligned leadership at all levels of the organization. That is why, in a foundational sense, the Virginia Mason story is a leadership story.

As Patterson says, at Virginia Mason *you see* leadership every day at all levels. "Leadership defies a single definition," says Dr. Kaplan. "It's elusive and complicated. Leadership in some ways is getting to a point where you can actually have a management method—the readiness that's created. It is about change management and one of the questions is exactly what leadership is required to effect large scale change in an organization? In some ways leadership is about creating a sense of urgency, a shared vision, and aligned expectations."

Lynne Chafetz, general counsel, puts it this way: "We see leadership every day in the way we manage the organization—setting goals, identifying what is really going on in a work unit, at an organizational level, identifying priorities, and holding ourselves accountable." Leadership is knowing that before defining organizational goals for the year, it is essential to go out into the organization to seek the ideas and thoughts of thousands of workers at all levels of the organization—an active "catchball" process that connects the front lines to the C suite. Leadership is visible in the bedrock understanding that the improvement journey has no end.

While more and more organizations are turning to lean management, many others are reluctant to do so, and Carolyn Corvi understands this. "When I first learned about the Toyota Production System and started to understand it, it just absolutely made so much sense to me. My reaction was why wouldn't you do this? It is so compelling because when you focus on quality everything else will follow. I think because it forces you to examine your work differently, people don't want to take the time to understand it."

While increasing numbers of leaders are adopting lean management, many others who could do so remain reluctant. The approach scares them. It is "foreign," too disruptive. There would be too much organizational resistance. Yet some of the most successful companies in the world—Boeing, Phillips, GE, Autoliv, Ingersoll Rand, Genie Terex, Caterpillar, Lego, WL Gore, Raytheon and others—rely on a lean management system. "I do think it requires a bit of a leap of faith," says Corvi. "It is not totally intuitive to everybody. You have to believe if you put this method in place you will get the kinds of results others have achieved. More importantly, it requires constant learning. You are always a student in the Toyota Production System."

Given the urgent need in the United States to create a health care delivery system that places a premium on access, quality, safety, patient-centeredness, and affordability, Virginia Mason offers a model for others to replicate. And the Virginia Mason model *can* be replicated by any health care organization with three basic characteristics:

- Leadership. As Carolyn Corvi says, "The leader has to be willing to learn. The leader can't sit back and direct it. You have to be out on the front lines of care. You have to understand the work. This is a real roll up your sleeves process."
- A workforce committed to putting the patient above all else.
- A willingness for all leaders to learn and apply the Toyota methods and tools. Health care, Corvi argues, has an inherent advantage in adapting lean methods. "You have to be a learning organization to make lean work and health care is already a learning industry," she says. "This culture of learning complements the Toyota Production System."

Already, hundreds of other health care organizations throughout the country have begun a lean journey, and for many the approach is paying dividends. Let's look back at what Virginia Mason board chair Young said near the start of the chapter: "I do not believe it is overly audacious for us to want to transform health care across the country." To some, perhaps, that reads as nothing more than bragging while to others it may seem naiveté. But in a way, this book serves to support Young's statement. Corvi certainly believes it:

> I remember the conversation we had with the board and executive leadership about our vision to be the quality leader and transform health care. We talked a lot about what that means. We *believed* in it then and we believe in it even more now. This idea really resonated with the board and leaders. We all agreed that if we're really committed to do this and do it right we will lead the transformation of health care. Somebody has to lead, so why not us?

Chapter 2

Strategic Plan
The Power of Alignment

If we are so focused on patients then how come all the systems are built around the doctors?

Katerie Chapman was fresh out of graduate school at the University of Washington and eager to channel her considerable energies into what would become one of the defining initiatives at Virginia Mason. Among her duties in the summer of 2001 was staffing a committee charged with no less than defining a future pathway for the medical center. The series of meetings, which included dozens of members of the upper echelons of management and the board, were focused on creating a Strategic Plan for Virginia Mason. Chapman was struck by how the board members—thoughtfully yet directly—challenged executives that the system at Virginia Mason was focused on patients. Senior executives were confident this was the case. Board members weren't so sure.

The question the board posed to the new leadership team was: *If we are so focused on patients then how come all the systems are built around the doctors?* This stung. The idea that the medical center was focused more on the needs and conveniences of the physicians and staff at the expense of patients was embarrassing.

The fact that leaders had not seen this clearly was more embarrassing still.

The board members were basically saying, 'If the patient comes first then why do you do some of the things you do?'" says Chapman. "And there was this silence. I don't think we had looked in the mirror. It was an assumption that if you are a health care organization *of course* you put the patient ahead of everything." That moment was something of a shock to the system, as surprising as it was troubling. "It was a humbling experience," recalls Sarah Patterson, "because we all assumed, 'Well of course you put the patient at the top,' but the board was really challenging us."

There are two particularly telling points here. First, there are some health care organizations—perhaps many—where board members would shy away from challenging senior executives, particularly senior executive physicians. The propensity for board members to defer to doctors is a long-standing tradition in many organizations. The second point, equally telling, is that in some other places—perhaps many—the senior leadership would push back and insist that they were a model of patient-centeredness. The leadership ethos at Virginia Mason is different. Board members, senior executives—all leaders—have built a culture where listening, learning, and facing the true nature of the current state are essential.

As a result of the board's challenges, senior leaders engaged in some soul-searching as well as observation to see that, in fact, Virginia Mason had a lot of work to do to become fully patient focused. And this notion became a key driver in the lengthy, often intense discussions concerning a new Strategic Plan they hoped would be characterized by wisdom, strength, and, perhaps above all, *sustainability*. Discussion, reflection, and debate stretched out over more than a year. Over time, the focus grew ever sharper.

What does leadership look like? This is a powerful example of assertive leadership by the board on behalf of patients: board members recognizing their primary allegiance to patients and having the confidence to raise a difficult, challenging question. From the standpoint of the executive team, what leadership looks like here is not countering the board's view but rather digging in to see what the reality truly was. This dynamic of leadership by board members and executive team—at all levels of the organization, in fact—has powered Virginia Mason forward.

"We went through quite a process," recalls then board chair Mark Hutcheson, "and produced this plan and one of the goals was to avoid this being just another sort of worthless planning process that resulted in a binder full of pages of materials… that people put on a shelf and all it does is gather dust. We looked at the prior plans. They were all too long. They were all too complicated." The goal was to create a plan that would play an *active* role in the organization for years to come. Once the individuals and committees had worked their way toward clear consensus on the essence of the plan, the next challenge was how to present it so that it could actually survive as a living document. This was no simple task as evidenced by the dust-collecting properties of old, well-intentioned Strategic Plans in many organizations.

"It was so clear at the time that they had this desire to create a Strategic Plan that resonated with people," says Chapman, "that people would *remember* and not be that 150-page document that sits in a binder on the CEO's credenza and is never looked at and doesn't *live* in the organization. It was so clear that the goal was to create a plan that would resonate with all the staff and that they could grab onto and say, 'I know what this organization is all about. I know where we're going and why.'" Chapman was a sponge in the meetings about the Strategic Plan. She was riveted by the nature of the discussion and writing down much of what was said. And as she listened to board members, senior executives, physicians, nurses, and others talk things through, she began to sort the material into general categories.

It Is Crystal Clear; There Is No Ambiguity. The Patient Is at the Top… Everything We Do Is Focused on the Patient

The job of presenting the essential themes of the plan in a manner that would be easy to understand and remember fell to Chapman along with Suzanne Anderson, then a consultant to the Virginia Mason board. The heart and soul of the plan was in putting patients first. Everything else in the plan was built to support this reverence for and devotion to the patient. Chapman and Anderson

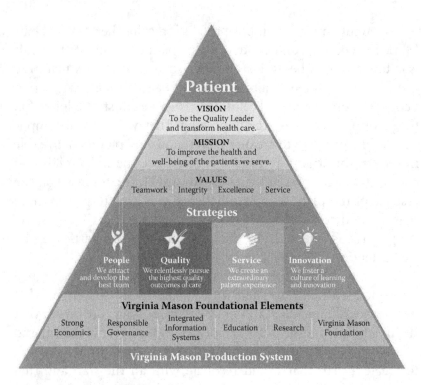

FIGURE 2.1 Strategic Plan.

worked the elements of the plan into a simple visual image of a pyramid with the patient at the top (Figure 2.1).

This Strategic Plan is alive, well, and thriving throughout Virginia Mason 14 years later, long past the life expectancy of most such documents. Physicians, administrative leaders, and staff members variously characterize the pyramid as *iconic, our map, a decision tool, a living document, rooted within the DNA of the organization, our shared vision*, and more. The image is ubiquitous throughout the medical center, and it is used as a starting point to guide virtually every meeting no matter the topic. It affects *everything* that happens at Virginia Mason. "It enables 5500 people to speak the same language," says Dr. Steve Rupp.

The essential power of the Strategic Plan is that it creates alignment throughout the organization. "It is crystal clear," says Dr. Donna Smith. "There is no ambiguity. The patient is at the top. It means everything we do is focused on the patient. It is true north." Although the plan is carried around as a laminated sheet of paper, it is more like a well-worn map or guidebook treasured by generations of explorers. It is called upon daily to guide discussions, to remind everyone what matters, as a map to show the way forward whenever there is confusion. "When conversations get squirrely in a conference room, someone inevitably will say, 'What is the best thing for patient?'" says Smith. "'If a patient were here, what would they say?' Or someone will point to the laminated copy on the table and say nothing. Or someone will say, 'That's not the best thing for the patient.' It gives permission to challenge others. In fact it encourages us to challenge one another because our direction is so clear."

Dr. Robert Caplan puts it this way: "Every time a conversation drifts toward convenience of staff it is self-correcting. The plan incessantly drives us away from self-interest toward the benefit of patients." The self-correcting nature of the plan equates the Strategic Plan to a simple yet reliable guidance system. In that respect it is somewhat analogous to the simplicity and reliability of a gyroscope, an instrument originally conceived in 1817 by Johann Bohnenberger, a German astronomer. It was later refined—as well as named—by the French physicist Leon Foucault, who found it useful in his effort to fathom Earth's rotation in space. Nearly two centuries later the gyroscope remains an indispensable device guiding some of the most sophisticated machinery known to man. It guides the Space Shuttle and serves to stabilize and guide the Hubble Space Telescope as well as the Russian Mir space station. It even guides the Mars Rover, 35 million miles away.

Like the gyroscope, the Strategic Plan serves to maintain the orientation of Virginia Mason and to keep it on course. Although the plan is a lot younger than the gyroscope, it nonetheless has served as a foundational system for Virginia Mason for nearly 14 years—a lifetime as these things go.

You've Got to Live This Every Day and If You Think ... We Don't Need to Do It You're Wrong

What does leadership look like? You can see it in the manner in which a major change in direction embodied within the Strategic Plan was rolled out within the organization. It was done with discipline and clarity so that leaders spreading the word of the plan to their teams speak the same language; emphasize the same essential points.

"We were issued a deck of slides about how to introduce the Strategic Plan, how to talk about it," says Patterson. With all leaders talking about it in the same way a sense of clarity developed. It was not long into the introduction before it was clear to every Virginia Mason employee that the patient was at the top of the new pyramid and that the patient was supposed to come first in everything always. "As leaders we were all talking about it in the same way," says Patterson. "We weren't going out and saying, 'Well, here's *my* view of this.' It was disciplined and rigorous." Patterson told team members throughout the organization that 'you've got to live this every day and if you think it's beneath you or you think, 'Well, we don't need to do it,' you're wrong."

The overall message was: Patient first, always, in everything. And every other aspect of the plan was in place to support that mission. "Presentations were scripted, and we didn't deviate," says Dr. Michael Glenn, chief medical officer. "You have to have a lot of rigor around the message with something that important." Patterson recalls that at the start the scripted messaging seemed a bit forced, but over time she says it has become an easy and natural part of the way people at Virginia Mason converse and "leads to incredible conversations within teams about how and what they are meeting about or working on and relates it directly to the patient."

The Strategic Plan resides within the core of Virginia Mason. It is among the most important tools—perhaps *the* most important—that leaders throughout Virginia Mason have to create alignment within the organization. "As a leader," she says, "you can be so much more effective when you know—and everybody else knows—what the vision and mission are and that is exactly what the plan gives us. The Strategic Plan makes clear that *we exist because of the patient*. It is very clear as our map. It's fabulous. As a leader I know exactly what our work is every day and that is *huge*."

The cultural shift at Virginia Mason did not happen overnight. As carefully planned and crisply rolled out as the plan was, it would take years before it could safely be said that the culture of Virginia Mason had evolved into a relentless focus on the needs of the patient.

As is clear from Figure 2.1, there is a larger story within the pyramid that supports the patient first commitment. Strong economics and financial health are foundational to be able to serve patients. To say responsible governance is important is to state the obvious in view of the fact that it had been the board in the first place—acting assertively—that initiated the design of the Strategic Plan. Central to the plan are the values that have come to be known within Virginia Mason as TIES: Teamwork, integrity, excellence, service. With the patient at the top of the pyramid and the Virginia Mason Production System as the foundational base, these values are steady guides "that speak to our values and connect everything we do," says Dr. Catherine Potts.

Dr. Joyce Lammert observes that during a recent retreat with hospitalists the doctors spent hours talking about their values, "and at the end of the day when they were summarizing them it turned out that it was really TIES," says Lammert. "It was all around teamwork, integrity, excellence, and service, and I thought, 'Wow, this is really working because here they are talking about what's important to them and is also what we are as an organization.'"

There have been discussions about updating the plan a number of times through the years. In 2008 board members and executives, upon reviewing the plan, noted that the plan element "People: We will recruit and retain the best physicians and staff" seemed insufficient. Alternatives were discussed, including the following:

We will attract and develop the best diverse team for our patients.
We will recruit and retain the best people.

The leaders in discussion noted:

Diversity is a core strategy that is not reflected in the Strategic Plan. Make it explicit on our strategic pyramid. Revise the Strategic Plan to reflect the team approach, i.e. not separating out "physicians" and "staff" and reflect that we want to recruit and retain the best people. "Recruit and retain" is reflective of our strategies vis-à-vis our employees but does not reflect our entire workforce. Consider going beyond "recruit and retain" and reflecting that we want our people to be "developed" and "engaged."

During the 2009 review the sense was that the element of the plan stating "Service: We will Unequivocally Insist on Extraordinary Patient Service" was changed to "We will create an extraordinary patient experience." The item indicating "Innovation: We will Promote a Culture of Innovation" was revised to "We will foster a culture of learning and innovation."

The board's discussion notes around this reveal the detailed review of every aspect of the plan:

> Should the Strategic Plan reflect a culture of learning organization as part of "innovation"? Innovation builds on kaizen "continuous improvement" and on a foundation of standard work. Innovation is a critical pillar … when making resource allocation decisions and has an important role in recruitment.
>
> Should innovation be a value or a strategy? It was noted that if it is a competitive advantage to serving our patient and achieving our mission and vision, it should remain a strategy. It is important to have a strategy supporting the adoption of disruptive technologies and processes (including, for example, the Virginia Mason Production System and the Center for Healthcare Solutions).
>
> "Promote" was felt to be a weak word; consider revising to "embed." How is innovation measured? Idea system? Specific changes in clinical processes? Medical "firsts"? Innovation should be retained as a pillar, and "learning organization" concept should be added.

Visible across the bottom of the pyramid—serving as the base of the image and the foundation of the Virginia Mason approach—is the Virginia Mason Production System, a lean management method derived from the Toyota Production System. It is this management system for which Virginia Mason is best known throughout the world of health care and as the base of the pyramid it is the unshakable foundation upon which the Virginia Mason transformation is constructed. (The management method is discussed in greater detail in Chapter 3).

To Be the Quality Leader and Transform Health Care

The most significant change to the Strategic Plan came in 2008 when the board enhanced the aspiration from being the quality leader to also seeking to transform health care. Was this an act of hubris? Arrogance? Certainly it may have seemed that way to some people in health care. The very idea that a modest-sized medical center in the Great Northwest would enunciate an aspiration to do no less than to fundamentally change the way medical centers operate and deliver care might have seemed something of a reach.

The document is in use throughout each day but it has become central to Virginia Mason's identity as teams gather for a wide variety of meetings and discussions. At the start of most of these sessions—the great majority, in fact—the leader will specify which elements within the Strategic Plan are most relevant for the particular meeting. The document is present both in its simple form as well as its role as a guiding aura throughout the organization.

Dr. Donna Smith says its omnipresence "keeps it alive and fresh in people's minds and reinforces alignment. It is woven into our fabric." During a planning meeting for a Rapid Process Improvement Workshop (RPIW), Lynne Chafetz started by connecting the work at hand with the Strategic Plan. "You might not think purchasing is related to the plan," she says, "but Legal Services provides support in reviewing contracts that provide the services, supplies, and equipment that are needed for patient care. This is a critical way in which we in legal services connect with patients and we have our internal stakeholders who need these goods and services to provide care to our patients. The Legal Department and Purchased Services are not in the frontline of patient care, but one of the things we try to do in the Legal Department is talk about: 'How do we simplify the process for the people who are at the frontline so that they have just what they need, when they need it, to be able to provide the care that we want to provide to our patients.'"

Alignment: Here Is My True North... This Guide, This Roadmap that Tells Me What I Should Be Doing

Alignment runs down the spine of the Strategic Plan; alignment around a common purpose, a set of shared values, goals, and methods of work. "As a leader, it gives you strength and courage to say, 'This is what we value,'" says Katerie Chapman. "'This is the way we are going to make decisions.' It's no longer, 'I've got to make a good decision as an executive. It's, 'Here is my true north and I'm going to make a good decision because I have this guide, this roadmap that tells me what I should be doing.'"

In any kind of organization barriers to effective leadership are common, particularly in highly complex fields such as health care where there are countless continuously shifting parts. But the Virginia Mason experience and the experience of many complex businesses that have adopted lean management reveals that the lean methodology supports leaders in a variety of foundational ways. The Strategic Plan plays a central role in establishing a common language. The pathway could not be clearer. In an industry where the road ahead is often opaque or worse, Virginia Mason sees clearly that the process of continuous incremental improvement using lean tools is the route forward.

It is fair to say that a tradition in American industry has involved department heads in conflict over resources. So often still, the fight is for *my* department, *my* project, *my* team as though it is a zero-sum game where some departments win while others lose. This framework subsumes the good of the organization to the benefit of individuals and their departments. The agenda and mission of a silo within the larger organization trump the agenda and mission for the whole. This sort of culture fuels dysfunction throughout much of health care and it may be the rule rather than the exception. But the trend is against this self-centric culture.

The Strategic Plan allows Virginia Mason to enjoy shared focus throughout the organization. This is an elusive thing in business today, particularly in health care where fossilized siloes within organizations result in conflicting focus based on unaligned agendas. Common language, a clear pathway forward, and shared focus are assets for any leader or group of leaders. With these elements in place Virginia Mason has achieved a deeply powerful sense of alignment throughout the organization. Alignment runs from the *patient at the top always in everything* to shared compensation to a goal-setting process that reaches across the organization. As one Virginia Mason leader after another echoes, "We are all on the same page."

"This isn't about talking points," says Dr. Michael Glenn. "We are all telling the same story because we are all focused on and living the same story. And everybody here can explain it to you." The plan has penetrated the broad Virginia Mason psyche and culture so thoroughly that Glenn has a standing bet that no one visiting the medical center can find an employee unaware that the patient resides at the top of the pyramid. He has never had to pay off on the bet.

Alignment Essential to Setting Organizational Goals

Each year, Virginia Mason leaders define a set of organizational goals. For several years after the death of Mary McClinton, there was but a single goal: to ensure the safety of patients through the elimination of avoidable death and injury. With significant progress on that front, the organization moved to defining a substantial number of annual, organization-wide goals. The process of establishing the goals is broadly inclusive and guided by the Strategic Plan. An environmental scan—both internal and external—kicks off the process. What are the internal strengths, weaknesses, and opportunities and what are the external or internal threats? What is the business environment? What are competitors doing? What changes are coming in the regulatory environment? A picture of the internal and external situation becomes clear and guides the decision making. Says Chafetz:

> One of the things that we've been able to do better and better every year is our goal-planning process. We have improved our ability to think about the many defects that present opportunities

for improvement. We have had really good discussions in the last couple years about understanding all the work going on across the medical center and aligning around our organizational goals. We've gone from a single goal about safety to multiple goals, so there's always this struggle of: How do we get down to the critical *few* goals but make sure that we're communicating to the organization the importance of all the work that we're doing. The Strategic Plan is the aligning document. We go through a process where we ask a lot of questions and listen to a lot of ideas. What's our current condition? What are our aims for the next period of time? How are we going to measure that? Who needs to be involved? How do we ensure they know? And then we monitor that so we understand how we are progressing toward our goals.

This process is different from many other organizations in that once the goals are decided upon there is alignment throughout the organization to achieve the goals. This is not a case where the hospital goes off and does its thing or the clinic goes off and does something else. It's the whole senior leadership team coming together and agreeing on what the focus will be for the coming year. Debra Madsen, associate general counsel, says the Strategic Plan guides the goal development process where metrics measuring performance are defined in advance. It is a process that "ensures *breakthrough* improvements required for success and is critical to progress in achieving the Strategic Plan." Says Patterson, "Organizational goals are critical to executing on our Strategic Plan and achieving our mission to be the Quality leader and transform health care."

The goal-setting process overall is depicted in Figure 2.2. It is embedded within the Virginia Mason structure and culture. Foundational to the Strategic Plan, for example, are the following four pillars: people, quality, service, and innovation. Within each of those pillars are objectives aligned with organizational goals. Within each pillar, teams seek to identify where they want to be in five years and what it will take to get there. In doing so, the pillar plans include an overall goal as well as strategy, tactics, and metrics. As an example, human resources leader Kathy Shingleton and her team defined the goal for their five year *People* plan as

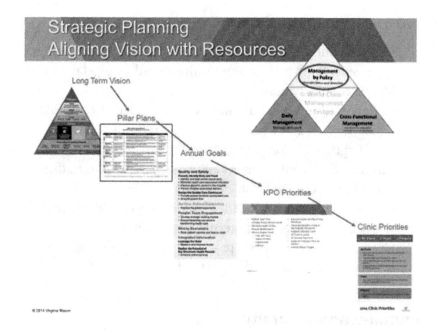

FIGURE 2.2   Aligning vision.

"Talent Acquisition and Workforce Planning—Ensure that the Right People are in the Right Role, at the Right Place, at the Right Time." Their strategy to reach the goal is defined this way:

1. To meet patient demand, create and implement staffing plans that include:
   a. Forecasting operators and competencies (knowledge, skills, and behaviors) needed across the organization to ensure that Virginia Mason has the requisite talent to meet the needs of our patients (2020 forecast & workforce planning).
   b. Create systems and processes to enable staff to flex between departments via standard work and cross-training (workforce mobility).
   c. Build internal and external applicant pipelines for critical positions (sourcing).
   d. Integrate staff into organization, department, or role.
2. Leverage Virginia Mason brand and culture (marketing).

And their tactics include the following:

1. Research and deploy tools to understand and predict staffing needs. Shift philosophy to hire ahead as top talent is identified and available.
2. Collaborate between human resources, Kaizen Promotion Office (KPO), and operations to ensure leaders have and use Virginia Mason Production System tools to design, execute, and continuously adjust departmental staffing plans to meet patient flow demands.
3. Create "competencies needed" models and address gaps with external hires and internal education.
4. Share and spread best practices around flexing staff between roles, tasks and departments, and so forth.

Sourcing and Diversity

1. Continue to utilize direct sourcing (proactively seeking talent), social media, and other online tools to attract and build relationships with potential applicants.
2. Deepen partnerships with educational entities and associations to build external pipeline for critical positions.
3. Develop inroads with key constituencies to increase the diversity of candidates presented for key positions.

Selection

1. Fully implement behavioral based interviewing to drive values based and bias-free selection.

Retention: Orientation and Onboarding

1. Provide standard tools for managers to provide comprehensive orientation and onboarding experience for new staff.
2. Refresh two-day organizational orientation for all new hires.
3. In partnership with staff relations conduct after action reviews on all early tenure turnover (see metric).

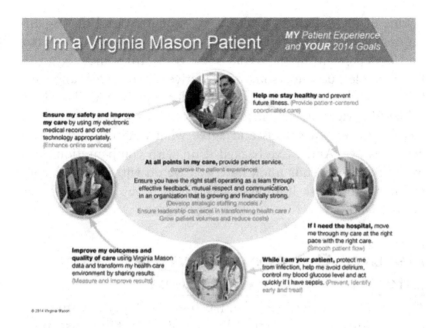

FIGURE 2.3   Patient point of view.

The metrics they identify to measure progress include reducing the "open position vacancy rate to 2.5% or less", increasing "self-reported diverse hires (race, age, military) by 5%", reducing early tenure turnover by 5%.

Several years ago a team created a visual to communicate goals to staff from the patient's point of view, thus showing a clear connect between the work of Virginia Mason teams and the needs of patients (Figure 2.3). For 2014, there were 12 organizational goals down from 15 the prior year. Examples of 2014 goals included under quality and safety are as follows:

- Identify and treat severe sepsis early
- Eliminate health care associated infections
- Improve glycemic control in the hospital
- Prevent hospital-associated delirium

Under strong economics was a single goal: "Grow patient volumes and reduce costs."

Under People: Team Engagement were two goals:

- Develop strategic staffing models
- Ensure leadership can excel in transforming health care

One of the defining aspects of alignment around the organizational goals is that every executive team member's compensation is dependent upon overall success toward achieving goals. For example, Sue Anderson, the executive vice president and chief financial officer, notes that "at the leadership team level we have achieved a view of the entire organization and we have worked hard to bring down silos and agree what our most important priorities are. And we've backed it up with compensation. Part of my bonus depends upon how well we do with glycemic control in the hospital. It allows us as a peer group to move in the same direction."

Natural Synergy: Strategic Plan and Physician Compact

The power of the Strategic Plan has been its ability to guide profound cultural change. It embodies a seminal shift in focus—from the doctors and staff to patients and families. This sort of change does not happen overnight. Highly trained health care professionals do not instantaneously alter the ways they have been performing. Cultural change stands as one of the most daunting challenges in health care or any industry for that matter and the Strategic Plan, at its core, serves as an engine of disruptive cultural change.

For decades, as was the case at many health care organizations, work revolved around the doctors, first and foremost, and then other staff members. Schedules, processes, management methods, and just about everything served physician preferences. For generations, this had seemed entirely sensible. The physicians, after all, were the men and women on a pedestal: brainy products of grinding years of medical school and arduous training. There was something magical about their skills and awe-inspiring about their knowledge. This physician-centric focus cemented itself into medical culture over many decades. A cultural tradition this deeply rooted is not easily disrupted.

Leaders at Virginia Mason were keenly aware of this fact during the development of the Strategic Plan. Thus, along with the Strategic Plan, the Physician Compact became a foundational element within Virginia Mason. To make the Strategic Plan work a new deal with physicians was necessary. If the old rules applied to doctors (e.g., entitlement, autonomy) then living up to the promise of the Strategic Plan would be unlikely if not impossible. In a sense, the Physician Compact cleared a pathway allowing the cultural shift embodied within the Strategic Plan. It helped to get the Strategic Plan off the launch pad. "We use the Physician Compact in a constructive and positive way to gain commitment from people," says board member Julie Morath. "The compact is powerful because it is reciprocal. It is not just a list of expectations. The reciprocity gives its strength."

Work to develop the Physician Compact was happening in about the same time frame as work to develop the Strategic Plan. Dr. Joyce Lammert and the members of the Compact Committee had hundreds, perhaps thousands, of conversations with physicians throughout Virginia Mason as they led the work to nail down what the "gives and gets" of the compact would be. This was an arduous process. Physicians were being asked to approach their work in a very different way in many cases. Says Lammert:

> We were really a physician-centered kind of place because the whole practice was designed around physicians. I think the compact, happening about the same time as the Strategic Plan, was like hitting the reset button. You have to change culture, but culture changes typically happen in an evolutionary way. The practice was formerly owned by the doctors and was a physician-centric organization. Since 2000 it has been a different construct. It is not a physician-run organization any more. It is an organization where a *team* takes care of patients. We couldn't have done the rest of the work over the past 13 years without the Compact.

At the end of the process to develop the compact—after 18 months of honest, sometimes raw conversations—it was time for the reset button. "The compact is very explicit about what the deal is now as opposed to what it used to be," says Lammert. "That doesn't change culture but it makes you have that discussion. And that's what was so important—that we really talked it all through and that we all understood once the Compact was agreed upon was: That was *then*, this is *now*" (Figure 2.4). While the Strategic Plan was completed ahead of the compact, there was

Virginia Mason Medical Center Physician Compact

Organization's Responsibilities	Physician's Responsibilities
Foster Excellence	**Focus on Patients**
• Recruit and retain superior physician and staff	• Practice state of the art, quality medicine
• Support career development and professional satisfaction	• Encourage patient involvement in care and treatment decisions
• Acknowledge contributions to patient care and the organization	• Achieve and maintain optimal patient access
• Create opportunities to participate in or support research	• Insist on seamless service
Listen and Communicate	**Collaborate on Care Delivery**
• Share information regarding strategic intent, organizational priorities and business decisions	• Include staff, physicians, and management on team
• Offer opportunities for constructive dialogue	• Treat all members with respect
• Provide regular, written evaluation and feedback	• Demonstrate the highest levels of ethical and professional conduct
Educate	• Behave in a manner consistent with group goals
• Support and facilitate teaching, GME and CME	• Participate in or support teaching
• Provide information and tools necessary to improve practice	**Listen and Communicate**
Reward	• Communicate clinical information in clear, timely manner
• Provide clear compensation with internal and market consistency, aligned with organizational goals	• Request information, resources needed to provide care consistent with VM goals
• Create an environment that supports teams and individuals	• Provide and accept feedback
Lead	**Take Ownership**
• Manage and lead organization with integrity and accountability	• Implement VM-accepted clinical standards of care
	• Participate in and support group decisions
	• Focus on the economic aspects of our practice
	Change
	• Embrace innovation and continuous improvement
	• Participate in necessary organizational change

© Virininia Mason Medical Center, 2001

FIGURE 2.4 Physician Compact.

and remains a strong synergy between the two. Certainly the development of the Strategic Plan—and its clarity—helped spur the compact discussions. "Absolutely the Strategic Plan had an impact on the development of the compact," says Lammert. "They are our foundational building blocks." And Steve Rupp says, "The Physician Compact provides an important framework. It is a good framework, particularly because historically the physicians have been the entitled class."

Cathie Furman recalls the pivotal nature of the compact particularly in light of the organization's later shift toward a more rigorous form of standard work. "We were starting to do something very different and we needed to be sure the physicians would be onboard," she says. "There was a lot of discussion at the time in health care about cookbook medicine versus evidence-based medicine. We focused on standard work as the foundation of clinical care. Creating agreements about a standard approach helped inform the best approach so all of that had to tie in together for us to move forward getting the consistency we needed."

What does leadership look like? Difficult, honest discussions define a vision and method for achieving that vision. The intense dialogue with doctors over a new approach to providing care happened during a turbulent period. Getting the work done, having the conversations, taking the time needed to engage with physicians, taking the time to listen, creating two simple documents (single-page pieces of paper that endure as though made of steel)— that is what leadership looks like.

Chapter **3**

New Management Method, New Ways to Lead

Ice in His Veins

On the evening of November 29, 2000, Volney Auditorium at Virginia Mason was packed with doctors, many of them red-faced with anger (fury was more like it). One physician grew so enraged he strode to the front of the room, interrupted the chairman of the board and the chief executive officer (CEO), and demanded to be heard.

This uncharacteristic hostility came in reaction to news that the Virginia Mason board had voted to radically alter the organization's governance laws. No longer would physicians have the power to elect the CEO. Instead, physicians would have no say in the matter. The CEO would be appointed by the board. This break with decades of tradition stunned many of the doctors in the room. It was particularly striking in light of the fact that only months earlier these physicians had elected Dr. Gary Kaplan as CEO and now he had supported a change depriving doctors of the right to vote. The anger resulted from what felt like a naked act of betrayal from a man who had long been well liked and respected by his colleagues.

"This is a betrayal!" several shouted at Kaplan.

"How dare you!" shouted another.

Physicians stood and screamed at him.

Not only had Kaplan and the board deprived doctors of the right to select a CEO, but the new governance rule also deprived physicians of the right to vote for section heads and department chiefs. Dr. Robert Mecklenburg, for example, had been elected chief of medicine by the physicians in the Department of Medicine, and each chief and section head was elected by physicians in that particular section. No longer. Now all chiefs would be appointed by the CEO, and all section heads appointed by their chiefs.

Dr. Kaplan and board chair Mark Hutcheson stood at the front of the auditorium explaining that the old system was outdated and did not adequately serve the needs of an organization that needed to make important changes going forward. But this only further enraged numerous doctors. Kaplan anticipated the reaction; he knew these men and women well. He knew they would be angry with him, but he also knew that change was urgently needed. The health care environment was rapidly changing, and Virginia Mason had to change with it. Eventually, Kaplan believed, Virginia Mason would get ahead of that change. He believed there was zero chance of that happening if the election process were maintained.

Throughout the turbulent session Kaplan remained composed. He neither raised his voice nor responded to insults. He explained that he believed the changes were essential for Virginia Mason's future. Mecklenburg had never witnessed anything quite like this: normally composed, even reserved, colleagues were leveling withering criticism at the new CEO. At one point when the tension seemed to reach a peak, Mecklenburg whispered to Dr. Michael Glenn seated next to him: "Man, Gary's got ice in his veins!" Recalls Dr. Steve Rupp, "It was a major moment in courage.'"

And it was a moment when a number of physicians—those sitting quietly in the audience—differed from their angry colleagues. These doctors welcomed the kind of change Kaplan envisioned. Other physicians were there to listen and consider the governance changes in a thoughtful way. One young physician spoke up and said he didn't care about having a vote. What he wanted, he said, was to work in a well-run organization with effective leaders who would be there over the long term. Kaplan knew he had the support of a contingent of doctors present. And he knew those doctors recognized that the future would be different—that significant change was needed. There was also a group of well-respected physician leaders at the front of the room—supportive of the changes—and that was a powerful, visible statement of their belief that this was a good thing for the organization.

The dissenters, however, were not done. A few days later a delegation of three physicians met with Kaplan in his office. One of the qualities that had enabled Kaplan to win election as CEO was his steady, calm demeanor. For example, no one at Virginia Mason had ever heard him raise his voice—until, that is, the three dissenters sat down in his office. "If you go through with this," one of the doctors threatened, "there will be a physicians' union in here soon." Kaplan exploded. He pounded his fist on the table and shouted, "If that is the only thing you three came here to talk about you can leave now!"

What does leadership look like? Often, as we have noted, it looks like alignment, the absence of siloes, teamwork, an efficient process. But sometimes it looks very different from those things. Sometimes it looks like a leader willing to do something difficult and unpopular because he is convinced it is best for the organization in the long run. Sometimes it looks like a leader putting the future of the organization ahead of his own popularity—even ahead of friendships.

The governance change was triggered by a question the board posed to Kaplan: What can we do to help you be successful? His response: Make the CEO position appointed rather than elected. He knew he was wading into perilous water, but he believed that "running for reelection every three years places huge political constraints on your ability to change because of the change-averse nature of so many professionals including physicians. We knew significant change needed to happen. There was leadership change for the first time in 20 years and some of us felt that elected physician governance was a weakness in the system, and we had felt that for a while. You could make a case that it was overdue in an organization like ours." The board agreed.

While electing leaders was a long tradition at Virginia Mason, those elections brought a natural tendency for leaders to think first about their constituency rather than about the organization as a whole. It caused leaders to tend their turf on behalf of the people who had elected them, thus pitting departments against one another competing for resources. It balkanized the organization—the antithesis of the alignment Kaplan believed Virginia Mason needed.

For all the anger, Kaplan had support from a number of other doctors who believed that he was on the right track, that disruptive change was needed, and that the governance change would enable Kaplan to do what he needed to do without being hampered by internal political considerations.

It's Been Successful, but Back Then We Didn't Know

This was a period of unprecedented turbulence at Virginia Mason. Barely four months after the fractious gathering of physicians, feelings still raw, Kaplan was quietly exploring the Toyota Production System. "The first time Gary talked about it to the team internally, we were given Polaroid cameras and told to go out into the hospital for 15 minutes and take pictures of waste," recalls Dr. Joyce Lammert. "So I went into the hospital and watched a nurse try to get a drug for a patient in a room. I could see her check the order, and she went into the room and couldn't get the thing open. And it turned out that there wasn't any drug, and then she had to call down to the pharmacy. I was there for about 30 minutes, and the patient still hadn't gotten the drug. And I remember it to this day because the light bulb went on—the waste was so obvious. It was the moment for me when I understood the importance of what we were about to commit to." Charleen Tachibana recalls those early exploratory days that seemed so daring. "It's been successful but back then we didn't know and we didn't talk to anybody even to our families about what we were doing," she says. "We didn't talk to anybody. There was just no way I could explain this to my husband, and he's in health care."

By the end of 2001 Kaplan and his leadership team had invested significant time studying the Toyota method. During that period, Kaplan had also done a good deal of exploring throughout the country. He visited a number of prominent health care organizations looking for a management method that might enable Virginia Mason to reach new heights. But he found nothing that he believed was right. Yet the more he and his colleagues read, studied, and discussed the Toyota Production System, the more convinced he became that it was right for Virginia Mason.

The great leap of faith came in June 2002 when Kaplan announced that the top 30 leaders in the organization would be traveling to Japan for an immersive two weeks of work at Toyota. And Kaplan made it clear to his leadership team that anyone wishing to continue in a leadership role at Virginia Mason was required to participate in the Japan trip. A few executives chose to leave rather than embark on the Toyota journey. Criticism of the Japan trip came from many quarters. It was an easy target for the press: "You're in financial trouble, yet you are taking 30 people for a three-week junket to a Japanese auto maker to learn how to improve the delivery of health care!"

Public ridicule was embarrassing, yet more disturbing was deeply felt internal dissent among physicians. Many doctors greeted news of the Japan trip with utter incredulity. As Kaplan and his team were becoming deeply enamored of the Toyota approach while in Japan, back in Seattle incredulity turned to hostility when the delegation returned from Japan and formally announced that Virginia Mason would adapt the Toyota Production System to health care as the organization's management method. This declaration caused a few physicians to leave Virginia Mason while many others were convinced Kaplan was destroying the institution.

"We had barely started, and it was already a difficult road," recalls COO Sarah Patterson. "People would say, 'You've lost the battle.' They would openly say that they were waiting to see if we would blink. Staff members would tell me that they were waiting us out. One doctor said to me, 'I'll give you two or three years, Sarah, and then if we're still doing this, I'll believe it and I'll get onboard.'"

Leadership at Virginia Mason is marbled throughout the organization, and, as we have noted, the vast majority of the time you can see leadership in a process, in a kaizen event, in standard work, and in executive rounding. In rare instances, however, a different type of leadership is required: leadership from a strong individual with the vision to see what needs to be done and the courage to implement it, however unpopular it may be in the moment. This was one of those times. "If you don't have the CEO pushing it, I would be shocked if you could ever get there," says Dr. Fred Govier. "You cannot do what we have done if it's not the CEO driving the work."

Bet the Farm Strategy

The first year of the Toyota work was done quietly, but after just shy of two years' work, Kaplan believed they had enough material and experience to share the basics with others in the vanguard of the health care improvement movement. The obvious place to do that was at the annual forum sponsored by the Institute for Healthcare Improvement (IHI). A leader in the improvement and innovation movement, IHI's annual forum attracted several thousand health care leaders from throughout the world.

Kaplan and then Virginia Mason president Mike Rona presented to a select group at the IHI CEO seminar, a subset of the forum. They explained that they believed the Toyota approach, based on eliminating waste as the route to quality, could work in health care. They reported on their trip to Japan and presented data from several kaizen events that had been conducted at Virginia Mason. The reaction from those in the room was mixed at best. James Womack, founder of the Lean Enterprise Institute and a leading international expert on lean management, was skeptical. The message from Womack and others seemed to be that this was too difficult to pull off in health care.

Diane Miller, Tachibana, and other members of the Virginia Mason team were taken aback by the reaction from many in the room. This was an audience of self-selected members of the health care improvement community, and Tachibana said she expected support for the direction Virginia Mason had chosen. Instead, some members of the audience expressed a sense of disbelief and even some mockery. "People were saying, 'You have got to be kidding! What a fool! What a *fool!*'" recalls Tachibana. "People were saying, 'I would *never* risk my career doing that. They're ridiculous.'"

Fortunately for Kaplan and his team, Paul O'Neill, former U.S. secretary of the treasury and Alcoa CEO was also in the room. He had become an expert in health care since founding and leading the Pittsburgh Regional Health Care Initiative, and he voiced immediate support for the direction Kaplan was leading Virginia Mason. In the face of skepticism from others, O'Neill's positive reaction buoyed Kaplan and his team.

While O'Neill's support for the approach was strong and has remained steadfast through the years, he uttered a phrase that day that stuck with Kaplan. O'Neill was clear that the stakes could hardly be any higher when he characterized Kaplan's approach as a "bet the farm strategy" on quality. O'Neill saw this as exactly the correct approach. He had been frustrated with what he saw as a "project approach to improvement" rather than having institutions commit to "habitual excellence." He later noted, "It is not possible to achieve lasting excellence side by side with business as usual practices. Over time systems revert to the mean."

Kaplan found the reaction sobering. "I got pretty nervous," he recalls. "It had a little bit of a ring to it—'bet the farm strategy.'"

There Is Hope and Optimism and a Sense that, Yes, We Can Do This

That moment in time—the unsettling feedback at IHI—proved relatively fleeting. Within the next year, there were indications that the management method could work. Improvement events suggested that the method enabled Virginia Mason teams to eliminate wasteful processes while improving the patient experience of care. Early on, for example, an improvement team found that nurses were spending less than a third of their time with patients. After a kaizen event in which various lean tools were applied, nurses were spending 90 percent of their time with patients. This particular improvement event proved to be an early touchstone. The Toyota tools had provided very specific data measuring what nurses did at any given time. They measured how far they walked during the day and, most important, the amount of time nurses spent with patients versus time spent looking for supplies and equipment and attending meetings, among other things. The finding that nurses were spending such a small amount of their shift actually attending to patients was startling. Once the reality of the current state was revealed, the tools helped the team alter the process for nurses, which enabled them to spend a great deal more time with patients. This change resonated throughout the medical center and helped capture the attention of many clinicians who had previously expressed skepticism about the Toyota methods.

In oncology, another improvement team found that ambulatory cancer patients—some of the sickest patients visiting Virginia Mason—were wasting many hours waiting for various aspects of care. Teams also found that these cancer patients, for whom time was their most precious commodity, were not only waiting hours for appointments and treatment but also wandering around the Virginia Mason campus in a crazy quilt pattern that served no purpose other than to exhaust patients.

The lesson from these events was just what Kaplan and the board had talked about soon after he had become CEO: That the systems at Virginia Mason were built around and for the convenience of providers and staff—not around and for the benefit of patients. But now the new management method and the tools it provided were enabling Virginia Mason teams to identify waste (anything that did not add value for a patient) and rebuild systems with the patient at the heart of the process. Thus, a new cancer center was constructed that brought virtually all services to the patient rather than having patients go from one area of the medical center to another to chase after treatment. The result was a meaningful decrease in wait times for ambulatory cancer patients and improvement in patient satisfaction. These and other events in the early years built momentum for the management method. On top of that, while the sense of skepticism among some providers and staff declined, a sense of confidence in the method increased. "Sometimes we'll be working on an RPIW, and it's day two of five and not going well," says Lynne Chafetz. "The team is falling apart, we're not coalescing around a good idea, and the people leading need to keep saying, 'Trust the process.' Be optimistic and keep persevering through, and then almost all the time it works. And that gives you cause for optimism."

As the years have progressed and Virginia Mason teams have engaged in thousands of improvement events, skill in the use of the lean tools has elevated to a level of expertise far beyond anything they were able to do in the first few years. And that expertise in combination with a belief in the system generates a powerful sense of optimism throughout the organization. The Virginia Mason Production System (VMPS) "absolutely gives you a sense of optimism that you can solve whatever the problem is and do it rather quickly," says Tachibana. "The management method and the tools work so well that there is always hope, and I think that is a key component of leadership—that there is hope and optimism and a sense that yes we can do this." Says Lammert:

> There is optimism because we have the tools to make it better. And instead of going, "Oh, woe is me, being a doctor isn't what it used to be," we can say, "Yeah, we've got the tools to make it better." I think it's sort of like having a vision. If you don't have optimism it can sometimes feel like a slog. But we have this optimism and a vision that we really *can* transform health care. And that's pretty amazing. The thing about the Virginia Mason Production System and leadership is that we have a common language we use that enables *everyone* to get involved. It helps people understand how to look at your work and how to improve your work in a way others will understand. The common language of VMPS is a unifying force that helps us visualize a value stream. It helps you realize that everything is connected along a patient's journey; that it is one continuous experience across the organization along a path that previously had siloes.

We Are All Held Accountable

The common language has been developed during the past 12 years and is perhaps never more evident than at Tuesday morning standup when various team members present updates on improvement projects. The session starts at 7:00 am sharp and is led by Kaplan. (When he travels, the session is led by Patterson.) Senior physicians, executives, and department heads suddenly appear in the long, narrow hallway a minute or two before 7, coffee cups in hand. This hallway tells the Virginia Mason story.

Along a 20-foot length of wall are charts, graphs, and numbers that indicate progress made—or lack thereof—on an array of essential metrics.

Members of the Kaizen Promotion Office step forward and succinctly report on where things stand with projects. These can be tense moments, particularly when a sticky project (i.e., an area that has been resistant to improvement) continues to show a lack of progress. There is no blame for individuals but the tension is there as is the pressure to perform. The tension rises one Tuesday morning when a KPO specialist reports that an effort to improve one of the clinical areas continues to go in the wrong direction, even after many months of work. A suggestion is offered indicating that perhaps a barrier to improvement has been the business of the winter flu season.

As the presenters report their numbers, Kaplan stands nearby taking notes. When they are finished reporting he reacts. On this particular morning he is frustrated with the lack of progress. He says that the explanation for why no improvement sounds to him a little bit like, "The dog ate my homework." His message is clear:

> While we are all busy and can all have reasons work is not completed it must be our commitment and accountability as leaders to see that the work is completed and to be on the genba and be removing barriers. We need to maintain our sense of urgency and not allow excuses to prevent our progress.

These sessions have been held every Tuesday morning for 12 years—52 sessions of accountability each year, 624 such sessions since Virginia Mason began its lean journey. As challenging as the Tuesday morning standup can be, Friday report-out sessions are more celebratory. "Tuesday morning is where the rubber meets the road," says Linda Hebish. "Friday report-out is designed to be a celebration of the work you have done with your team." Every Friday at noon—52 weeks a year for 12 years—teams present the details of successful improvement efforts that range far and wide across the organization from improving the efficiency of payroll delivery to reducing turn times in the operating room, from improvement in safety of medication distribution in the hospital to advances in efficiency in central processing. Says

Denise Dubuque, administrative director of surgical and procedural services:

> We are all held accountable for our work, and we hold ourselves and others accountable. At Friday report-out we celebrate and honor the work that has been done. And we all learn from the presentations. We learn how to apply the tools and methods by hearing others. It is also an opportunity to learn what we can just take and apply in our own areas. If I'm hearing something that might be applicable to work that I'm *doing*, I don't have to go out and redo it. This is knowledge that belongs to the organization. We want people to steal shamelessly.

Through the years at both Tuesday morning standup and Friday report-out—including more in-depth quarterly reports—Kaplan has made thousands of comments about a wide variety of the work. Details of his comments at a quarterly session in 2013 are revealing. "It really feels like things are coming together nicely," he says. He notes that the teams have taken on "an enormous body of work" that he finds "extremely impressive and I think we have a lot to be proud of. And we're getting better at being honest with ourselves." He comments briefly on a variety of topics raised during the report-out including work focused on more efficient payroll and access in the clinics. "When one patient has a bad experience, when they are unable to achieve the access or telephone contact or flow in the emergency room or one of our staff members is not getting the right paycheck that reflects on all of us. It's great to take time to really get under the hood and understand and make our processes more transparent," Kaplan tells the team. "We are a complex organization and we do well to recognize the complexity. We have to get even better at confronting it and creating standard work."

He is enthused by new improvement metrics on falls with injuries in the hospital. "A reduction of 39 percent is huge," he says. "That is having a great impact on our patients and their families." He applauds a 69 percent decrease in defects controlling patients' A1c and sees sepsis reduction as a "huge opportunity." The new Emergency Department (ED) has progressed significantly. "I hope people appreciate how far we have come with the ED. This is our front door and there is a real opportunity to make a dramatic impact." The ED improvement work reveals that "we have silos even within our service lines," he says.

Kaplan is delighted with the work that has resulted in improving patient access by opening clinics for full primary care services on Saturdays. "We need to make access bulletproof—to maternity leave or a provider leaving the organization. We shouldn't be at the mercy of an individual provider in unforeseen circumstances." He makes a particular point of emphasizing the importance of *nemawashi* and *speed*. Nemawashi is the term used to describe tilling the soil, getting people ready for change. "Nemawashi is very much about leader behavior, or preparing people," he says. "We've learned in the last five years how to make nemawashi come alive, and we will be able to move faster because of it. It takes time to prepare the environment, to get leadership in place. It's all about taking the time to prepare the environment to get leadership demonstrating the right behaviors."

Nemawashi is fundamental to the successful implementation of almost any change. "With nemawashi," says Patterson, "we engage the people who are doing the work. We get their ideas and we make sure they understand the need for change even before we do an improvement workshop in their area. We keep them updated during an improvement event so they know what ideas have been generated and tried and we make sure they have a chance to ask questions and express their concerns."

During the session Kaplan refers to what he calls his conflict of patience and impatience. "I've decided it's not a conflict any longer. It's actually the way it's supposed to be. Do the right work, prepare the people to pilot small tests of change but then we're supposed to take off and accelerate our process; part and parcel of the same work. As leaders, we need to be comfortable with that ambiguity. Maybe it's not ambiguity at all but clarity around the importance of pace and speed."

World-Class Management

Within Virginia Mason's DNA, one strand of the double helix represents VMPS, while the other represents world-class management. What, exactly, is the latter? It is a leadership system that provides focus, direction, alignment, and a method of management for daily work. Note that it is a *leadership* system and thus aligns with the *management* system that is VMPS. "There is a perception that the Virginia Mason Production System and lean management are the same thing," says Kaplan. "They are not. Our management system embraces lean tools but it is far more than that. In some ways it is world-class management."

This technique has been integrated into VMPS during the past several years to a point where it is essentially another way of defining VMPS. World-class management is composed of three interrelated components:

Management by policy: Provides focus, direction and alignment within the organization through a goal-setting process that engages everyone.

Cross-functional management: Involves improvement work across the organization focusing on breakthroughs within value streams that reflect the reality of how patients experience care across the entire system rather than in siloes. Aligns across the organization toward full customer satisfaction.

Daily management: Focuses on "how we do our work every day as leaders," says Patterson. Essentially standard work for leaders, the daily routines and behaviors of leaders from a frontline supervisor to an executive that create the environment and ensure reliability of processes day in and day out.

Says Linda Hebish, "The idea of daily management is let's fix it *in the moment.* Our vision is to go from firefighting to creating capacity so you can see what is coming down the pike."

An important element of the Virginia Mason culture involves a sustained search outside the medical center walls for ideas that might help improve management and the patient experience of care. A number of Virginia Mason executives dove into a book by organizational psychologist David Mann titled *Creating a Lean Culture: Tools to Sustain Lean Conversions.* Mann's book, a 2006 Shingo Prize winner, has helped guide the work at Virginia Mason and other organizations. (It is in its eight printing and is being translated into Chinese, Russian, and Thai.) Says Hebish:

Daily management, which is really leadership standard work, is considered by many people in manufacturing to be a game-changer, and I believe it's true. What better role model for frontline workers than leaders being present where the work is done—teaching, guiding, and coaching? Leaders are on the genba to coach, mentor, and improve daily work by reducing waste. The closer you are as a leader to the frontlines the more standard your work. World-class management and daily management in particular are game-changers because you are embedding accountability throughout your leadership team at all levels. You are seeing in real time what your production is today.

There is an important visual element to daily management. Wherever people go at Virginia Mason it should be clear what the unit does and where it stands in its work for that day at that moment. And when there is change—greater patient demand than anticipated, staff shortage, whatever it may be—the production board reflects that updated information so that everyone on the team knows what is needed *right now*. Is the team on schedule? Behind? If behind, then what is the standard work needed to catch up? This approach standardizes all day-to-day operations so that even if the leader is not present all team members know what to work on at any given time. Says Patterson:

> Leaders have two important jobs—running their business and improving their business, and they are right there side by side with staff doing the work. It's about working with people in a respectful way so they have the opportunity to identify the problems we need to fix through root-cause analysis. Then, for me as a leader to be right there asking questions, helping to be sure there are the resources to fix them. It isn't the leaders that are deciding what to work on, it's the people who do the work because they know what's getting in the way of providing great care to our patients.

Daily management strengthens standard work and reduces variability in day-to-day processes. A key part of leadership at Virginia Mason is making sure standard work is developed and followed for the benefit of patients. "This is what many organizations struggle with the most: how to ensure the improvements they have made are sustained," Patterson says. "Without leaders regularly checking to see if they are still in place and signaling that it is important to follow the new standards, it is easy for things to drift back to everybody doing it their own way." When Patterson is on the genba seeing the reality of the current state in the hospital or clinics, "I'm looking to see if I can see the standard work in place," she says. "The idea is not just to get a report from the person who reports to you, but to literally be there on the genba watching and looking, coaching, teaching. As an executive leader, I should not be just relying on my team to tell me what's going on but I should go out and see for myself."

Daily management means not only that leaders are following standard work but also that the notion of sticking to standard work is cascading down to all levels of leadership. Managers, for example, may be checking on standard work at least weekly and perhaps even daily. And Patterson says that at a supervisor level, "supervisors check in with their frontline staff on an hourly basis in some cases. Supervisors may round three or four times a shift, and they are continuously pitching in guiding, responding to questions and concerns."

Ideally, if daily management is in place and all leaders are doing their jobs, then Patterson says you should be able to see what any work unit does, whether it is on schedule, and more. "This is really how the culture shifts from those days of heroic action in health care to reliability and calm and providing great care every day," she says.

With standard work for leaders there is greater discipline and focus on anticipating the day's work. Huddles are essential in all work units so all team members are aligned. Key metrics are posted every day so there is visible evidence of how the unit is doing toward its goals. "We started doing huddles at production boards and reviewing key stats," says Patterson. "We encouraged the huddles and made clear that it was not okay *not* to do it. It enables people to really understand what's going on in your work unit and when that happens team members have ideas and we have the discipline and structure to implement those ideas. In addition to daily huddles it's important weekly during a huddle to review what's going on in our work unit that ties to our overall organizational goals. What are we working on related to patient satisfaction and quality and safety?"

World-class management did not take hold overnight at Virginia Mason. It took time before people had boards up in work units and, early on, staff members wondered aloud what the purpose of the quick daily huddles was. "But with huddles you now see the engagement of the staff," says Patterson. "Now I hear a lot about the huddles being critical and they happen even when a leader is out for the day. Staff members take the initiative to do it."

Sarah Patterson: A Leader's Voice

Patterson has led much of the world-class management work and has a developed a deep understanding of its power within Virginia Mason:

> It's creating leadership structures, discipline that allow you to execute it. It includes mission alignment, knowing what is important work that all leaders in the organization need to be supporting. It includes that daily management piece. What do I do every day as a supervisor that's going to ensure the patient care gets delivered and the improvements get added?
>
> It goes down to the level of huddles before every shift to get everybody aligned: here's why we're here, and here are the issues in our work unit. The rigor and discipline then creates the freedom to start to learn and change but you have to have that discipline in place.
>
> So there are huddles before every shift so every team member knows exactly what's going on. Those boards we have up that give the transparent environment so everybody knows, "Oh, I know on my unit we're really busy today and we're going to take these countermeasures. We're borrowing a staff person from somewhere else, and then here are our improvement efforts. Here's the stuff we're working on to make it better, and I'm engaged in that as a nurse or a Patient Care Technician (PCT).
>
> And then you move up the leadership line, and the next level leadership is checking on that work. They're saying, "That's really important work. I want to make sure it's on track, the work

of implementing standard work in your work unit or the roll-out of this. I'm here to help support that and I'm going to hold you accountable."

Charleen Tachibana does genba rounds in the hospital, and part of what she and her team are rounding on is the standard work that we've developed. It has to be in every unit, and what has I think amazed her and amazed me is it's taken years to develop the discipline of, "No, we really mean it and we mean it day in and day out." So there has to be this incredible rigor and discipline that then creates stability in the organization that people can do their jobs. They can handle changes being made to the work processes because everybody knows when they're going to get the information. Their leader, their manager, is there theoretically on the genba with them because we've redesigned their job so they can actually be with the people doing the work.

Do I give you the opportunity to identify the problems we need to fix and am I right there fixing them with you? Leaders don't decide which problems to fix. It's the people that do the work because they know what's important to the organization. The idea is not just to get a report from the person that reports to you but to literally be there on the genba watching and looking and saying, "Oh, I can see that we're following the standard work," and then it goes down to managers and could be as often as daily that the managers—it may be weekly a manager checks in with an administrative director, and then daily that a manager checks in with the supervisor who reports to them.

But I think that the key is the behavior we exhibit out on the genba. Are we out on the genba creating fear and blaming people, or are we out there truly modeling transparency? I want to know if there are problems. How can we work together? How can I help prioritize?

It's a lot of pick and shovel day in and day out really demonstrating to people you mean it. You're not just saying, "Give me your ideas." We got that feedback about a year and a half ago: "You say you want our ideas, but then my supervisor tells me that oh, yeah, he's already heard that before and has had that idea. That will never work. Or it's Oh, yeah, give us your great ideas and then we'll shoot them down." It's tough because it means every day you have to be modeling the behaviors that tell people yes, we do want their ideas. They are valuable to helping patients.

The Variation Itself
Kills the Product

Dr. Steve Rupp, medical director of perioperative and procedural services, could clearly see that throughout the department of anesthesia there was significant variation in how different doctors did their work. This sort of independence had long been essential to a physician's ability to do the work in the way he or she chose—typically according to their particular training. "You are taught in medical school to individualize anesthesia to every patient, and individualization creates the expectation that everybody can do whatever they want," says Rupp. "This embeds variation from case to case and provider to provider. The variation itself kills the product." What exactly does Rupp mean by this—that *variation kills the product*? Rupp explains:

> Patients get a wide variety of types of anesthesia, and some patients do very well after surgery: minimal pain, able to engage with physical therapy, and so forth. But many other patients suffer from a variety of ailments after surgery—vomiting, severe pain, somnolence, itchiness, and more.
>
> Some patients get general anesthesia, some get a spinal, while others get a spinal and a femoral nerve block and others get morphine. And the results when these patients reach recovery or get up on the ward are often unpredictable. Some do great while in some the pain is out of control. And a lot of this is due to variation in anesthesia. We created a standard pathway. We said, "Let's use the evidence and *apply* the best evidence we have and within rough parameters for the way we do a spinal block and femoral nerve catheter for total knees. This is big. To get to the standard pathway we had to challenge everybody to give up his or her autonomy to allow a better product. And that was a tough thing because everyone was taught that you can't do cookbook anesthesia.
>
> But we created a standard footprint around the patient for where the ultrasound machine goes, where the anesthesia tech stands, where the operator stands. We standardized the drugs to be used, including a multimodal pain relief regimen. For example, we used evidence-based medicine to select the best nonnarcotic drugs for pain relief. Now, there *are* some variations. For example, you can't give celecoxib to somebody who has sulfa allergy. Also,

the patient may be elderly, so we omit or reduce the dose of gabapentin because that drug can depress their level of consciousness.

But what this pathway allows you to do is actually manage the patient using state-of-the-art medicine—really focus in on the *key things* that are particular about this patient. If they have diabetes or if there is a cognitive problem, you can tailor the anesthetic within a framework. This produces a much more consistent outcome. Having reduced the variability in drugs and techniques, the quality of the product becomes much, much more predictable and much better. Finally, your ability to measure the outcomes and make changes to improve your pathway becomes much easier if there is a consistent baseline plan.

Drawing upon the collective wisdom of the 33 Virginia Mason anesthesiologists—identifying improvements from the people who do the work—Rupp and his colleagues sought to define precise protocols for a variety of surgical procedures. This work began in 2005 with the IHI initiative to establish widespread use of standard work for inserting central lines. Prior to this initiative from IHI there was widespread variation in how central lines were placed. The result was an epidemic of infections in those lines—a particular danger to seriously ill intensive care unit patients who require central lines. "This was part of the IHI 100,000 Lives campaign and we adopted that protocol," says Rupp. "And that was the start of getting our team to agree to using a particular pathway." This was not easy. A number of anesthesiologists pushed back pretty vigorously. A couple of others—decrying cookbook medicine—left the department for another medical center. Yet the early protocols worked well. And as variation narrowed patient care improved. Pain was reduced. Patients got to physical therapy more quickly.

In the ensuing years many members of the department of anesthesia proposed a protocol of standard work for various procedures and the group would meet to discuss those recommendations. "The person who wrote it would bring it to a department meeting and we would vet it and talk about it," says Rupp, "and the person who wrote it would listen carefully and make some adjustments and over time others would make suggestions for improvements and then we would have our standard work." While this work looks initially as though it is about anesthesia, it is just as much about leadership: working with 33 experts to lead them away from long-standing traditions to identify standard work. The instinctive resistance of physicians to standard work is well established. Yet here is an entire department where every anesthesiologist not only follows standard work for many procedures but also participates in identifying and sharing ideas for additional standards.

This is not a matter of doctors rolling over. This is not a case where standards are jammed down anyone's throat. This is a case where leadership at the top of the organization and within the departments has fundamentally altered the culture so that pursuing standard work is seen and accepted as part of the commitment to put patients first always in everything.

The leadership here is about culture, it is about the management method, it is about using science to identify the best way to do something and proving that to doctors doing the work. "The variation kills the product so once you agree and everyone is following standard work then whatever the problem may be pops out," Rupp says. "When there is variation in anesthesia and there are people up on the ward with a variety of reactions you can't tell what the problem is but if you are all doing it the same way and then you see the issue is vomiting then you can make an adjustment. You know what the issue is. When you agree to do it one way you can see the result—if nausea is a problem, for example, you can fix it and rapidly improve your protocol."

The lesson is about leadership creating the management method and culture to be able to identify and implement standard work. It's 33 anesthesiologists coming together and agreeing on very specific protocols for virtually every procedure in orthopedics and for many other operations as well. "It's been a huge, huge boon to patient safety and quality and empowerment," says Rupp. "Look at our patient satisfaction ratings from Press Ganey. We're in the top 1 percent in the country in the three key anesthesia measures."

You're Still Doing These Workshops?

An essential truth to VMPS is that the improvement work never ends. There is no target date for completing the work and declaring victory. Conveying this notion of infinite improvement in a very finite environment has not been easy, but over time it has taken root within Virginia Mason. Yet there are jarring moments when health care providers from outside the organization seem to not grasp this notion at all. Michael Glenn, chief medical officer, was providing a tour to a doctor from out of town and brought him to the accountability wall where Tuesday standup takes place. It is the place where metrics tell the true story of what is going on at Virginia Mason—successes and failures alike.

When the two men stopped in front of the wall, Glenn pointed out a couple of metrics as examples of the work:

> The other doctor looked at me and he said, "So you're still doing these workshops?" And I said, "Absolutely." And he thought that you've done all this work and wrote a book, and now you're like, "Hey, we're good. His attitude was, "Wow, you're still doing this? These charts are really detailed, aren't they?" I think people hear about the work, but they don't understand really what you're doing when you're talking about this. It's as though, "We're done, and we solved sepsis or whatever." It was a real revelation for him. And sometimes here we think everybody understands what you're doing and you realize some people have no clue.

If We Didn't Have VMPS Now I Would Be Terrified

A growing number of leaders in health care recognize the efficacy of the Virginia Mason approach. In the coming years, as leaders throughout the nation search for a pathway through the minefield that is modern health care, will there be a greater migration toward lean management? As we examine the trend it becomes clear that adopting VMPS—as the North Shore and Summit groups are doing in Massachusetts and Pennsylvania, respectively (details of both these stories in Chapter 8)—demands a courageous brand of leadership. It requires leaders willing to take the risk of shifting to a new and very different management system. It requires learning new tools—almost like learning a new management language.

For many leaders, the disruption is too great a risk. But for many others the risks of dramatic change will bring the kinds of rewards Virginia Mason enjoys: Improved patient experience of care, greater safety and access, rising physician and staff satisfaction, a stronger bottom line, and more. But as Virginia Mason leaders invariably tell people, it is not easy. And that alone is enough to scare off the timid. It all comes down to how leaders see the future. Does a particular leader believe, for example, that improvements at the margin will sufficiently stabilize market position in the future? Or does a particular leader see a radically shifting landscape where a quality strategy is the only pathway forward?

Joyce Lammert believes that the constant going forward from health care organizations will be, among others, an aggressive pursuit to eliminate waste. "Understanding waste and working to eliminate it has never been more relevant than it is now," says Lammert. "The reality in light of the reimbursement situation is that you cannot survive in next few years if you cannot get waste out of your system. If we didn't have VMPS now I would be terrified."

Chapter 4

Respect for People

Essential to the Virginia Mason Production System

Wow, How Shallow Are We?

In an immaculate area within a Hitachi manufacturing facility in Japan, two Virginia Mason teams worked honing their lean management skills by identifying waste in the Hitachi production process. A series of well-spaced white stripes looking something like yard lines painted on a football field separated the two teams. The lines were spotless high-definition white. The senior sensei informed the teams that they should work within the lines. "He said, 'You can stand on *that* side of the white line, or you can stand on *that* side of the white line, but you must not stand *on* the white line,'" recalls Charleen Tachibana, a team leader. "And we would go about our business and every so often he'd come up and say, 'You're on the white line. You can stand on that side or that side but you don't stand on the white line.' And he was being kind of a pain in the butt about it."

Dr. Lucy Glenn, the other Virginia Mason team leader, says that "the sensei kept reminding us not to step on white line and we would get caught up in the work and forget. He would remind us multiple times and most of us felt this was a little ridiculous.

On the second day the sensei came to me and he explained that the supervisor cleaned the white lines every night. He did it out of respect for his staff—making sure his staff could see the white lines so they could see the safety zones." Some of the lines served to mark pathways where heavy carts ferried equipment and any worker in that area could potentially become injured. "When I relayed this to the team," says Glenn, "they then understood the importance of not stepping on the lines and we decided as a gesture of respect to get down and scrub the white lines."

Unaware of this explanation, Tachibana was flabbergasted when she looked over and saw Glenn and her team on their knees. "I look across, and Lucy's team is on the floor and they're scrubbing the white lines, I had no idea what was going on, but it was clear he was *obsessed* with the white lines." After a time, the sensei approached Tachibana. "You understand the white line, correct?" he asked her. "No, I don't understand the white line." And he said:

> "You do not stand on the white line out of honorable respect for the person who painted it." He noted as well that the safety of workers depended upon the lines being bright and clean. So every time we stood on the white line it showed disrespect for workers' safety and for the people who had painted the lines so precisely. The painters had taken pride in their work and done an excellent job, and we were dishonoring their work by unnecessarily stepping on the lines. The painters were invisible to us. It was really startling to me. I thought, "Wow, how shallow are we?" And I realized that we did not see all those invisible people just as we did not see invisible people back in our own organization—that we had no appreciation for what they do. They are *invisible* to us really.

Invisible Workers

Millions of workers throughout the United States are invisible in this way. Throughout an array of industries many workers' efforts receive little or no appreciation or respect, and Tachibana realized that the same held true at Virginia Mason. There were invisible employees whose excellent work and dedication to the mission went unappreciated or certainly underappreciated. For example, deep in the bowels of the hospital, workers labored 24 hours a day, seven days a week sterilizing surgical instruments. Yet in spite of the critical importance of their duties these workers were, in a certain respect, invisible. Says Tachibana:

> These workers are chipping blood off of surgical instruments and they are invisible to the vast majority of the organization. They're invisible. So the white line was a stunning story for us and for those of us on that trip it was the story we told when we got back home. It had a profound impact on many of us. We really questioned ourselves. How much do we really understand *everybody* who contributes in this organization and the contribution they make and the work that they do?

Sterile processing workers in the basement stand over sinks washing and then decontaminating scopes, retractors, scalpels, and countless other instruments. They feed instruments into a sterilizing machine and then assemble the instruments into pans, each containing approximately 65 instruments. At Virginia Mason, approximately 1,000 pans are sent up to the operating rooms and other procedure rooms every day. Yet here is the rub, the white line disrespect factor: On average, 60 to 70 percent of the 52,000 instruments cleaned each day are never used. Thus, workers are cleaning upward of 35,000 instruments every day that are sent to the operating rooms and then sent back unused to be cleaned and sterilized all over again. Of course, there is a certain unpredictability concerning what instruments exactly will be used during a procedure, but it is far from *that* unpredictable, says Denise Dubuque, administrative director of surgical and procedural services, who is working to correct this wasteful process. "We believe it is disrespectful to have our staff members cleaning and assembling instruments that were never used in the operating room," she says, "and it is our challenge to fix this as quickly as we can."

There Is Bullying in Health Care and You Have to Commit to Respectful Behavior

Respect for people is a core tenet of the Toyota Production System, but it was an aspect of the methodology that Virginia Mason had not focused on much while working on the methods and tools to reduce waste while improving quality, safety, and affordability. But the white line story—the waste of workers efforts in sterile processing and other instances of disrespect—took a cumulative toll. While physicians and other staff were relentlessly patient-focused, they were not always respectful of one another. Staff members were frustrated when they felt marginalized and not listened to. In one example, a surgeon prescribed a certain medication for a patient. A team member spoke up and said she thought it seemed like a large dose and perhaps they should check with a pharmacist. While the dose was unusual, the surgeon had very carefully calculated it and knew it was correct. Nonetheless, the staff member was doing precisely what she should do to protect the patient: calling out the fact that the dose was unusual. But the surgeon didn't like it, and he snapped at the staff member: "Where did you get your medical license from?"

In an ideal culture this would have worked out quite amiably, but it ended with an awkward breach between the surgeon and the staff member. Would the person speak up next time to raise a safety concern? Would others who had witnessed the exchange speak up or would those staff members be reluctant to say something for fear of humiliation? "We learned that until you actually dedicate yourself to respect for people in the workplace you are going to be hampered," says Dr. Steve Rupp, medical director of perioperative services. "You have to commit to respectful behavior. Because the fact is, there is bullying in health care—bullying of residents, bullying within nursing groups, tech groups—it is a reality."

Ilana Yurkiewicz of Harvard Medical School described the sometimes bullying nature in health care in an article in *Aeon Magazine* focused on an organization other than Virginia Mason:

> He comes to the operating room late, greets no one, and berates the nurse for not setting up the stepstools the way he likes. He tells the resident she doesn't know the anatomy and sighs when she adjusts her grip on a surgical tool. He slaps the hand of the medical student when she reaches for the retractor to pull back skin for a clearer view. The operating room is tense for hours. "I need a different clamp," he says at one point. "This one is too

dull." Says the scrub nurse, "I'm on it." He retorts, "You're not, or else it would already be in my hand." All of us adorned in blue scrubs and surgical caps stand on edge, braced against the next wrathful outburst. "I want to see the tip of my blades," the resident explains, staring intently at the monitors where her laparoscopic instruments have not quite come into view. *"Just cut,"* the lead surgeon barks at her. By the end of the operation, the intern's hand shakes as he sutures the wounds closed, to the beat of the running condescending commentary on his halting speed and less-than-perfect stitches. ["Medical disrespect: Bullying doctors are not just unpleasant they are dangerous. Can we change the culture of intimidation in our hospitals?"]

Our Goal Is to Have a Team that Feels Respected and Valued and Heard.

In 2010, Virginia Mason introduced service training throughout the organization in an effort to improve service to patients and families. All Virginia Mason employees enrolled in a basic training class focused on specific steps workers could take to improve service. While the training proved quite effective, there was a revealing by-product that emerged from it. Employees said, "Yes we need exceptional service for patients, but we also need to work on how we treat each other." Says Katerie Chapman, "People started saying, 'Boy, I wish people treated *me* the way we're trying to teach them to treat patients.'"

These are perilous waters for any organization. However, for one dependent upon ideas and innovation from frontline staff, this is a flashing red warning signal. Lean management cannot function without full-throttle commitment from workers at the front lines, for the inherent strength of the method lies with the engagement of these workers. It is the people who do the work who redesign and improve the work because they know it best. "It means every day as leaders we have to be modeling the behaviors that tell people, 'Absolutely, we want your ideas,'" says Sarah Patterson. "'We need your ideas and we will implement your ideas.'"

The feedback mounted with increasing numbers of employees sending the message: *Service training was great but we really need some kind of training about how we treat each other.* "Our goal is to have a team that feels respected and valued and heard," says Chapman. "And one of the questions was what would success look like? And one of the team members said, 'Well, if I felt respected and valued in this organization, you would get better equipment for smoke evacuation in the OR.'" This struck Chapman. "This was so important because when you're cauterizing, you're producing a plume and they don't want to breathe it in. And I thought of course! Why would I ask you to breathe in the exhaust?"

"If you look at the literature about Toyota, Respect for People is a core component of the philosophy," says Lynne Chafetz. "So I think we've been talking about respect for people since we adopted the management method without articulating it in those words."

This notion was ever present when Virginia Mason teams visited plants in Japan. Working in a Toyota plant Jim Cote, senior vice president and clinic administrator, could see by the actions of managers that "the system is all about respect for the employee. Managers are right there with the workers to help, coach, and teach. It is genuine respect in action." Says Chapman:

> If you're asking people to invest and engage and change, they've got to feel safe to do so. They've got to feel valued and respected, and if you haven't had those foundational things in place they feel threatened. They feel like they've got an unsafe environment— maybe it's hierarchical—the ORs are known for being very hierarchical. *Why would I speak up for safety?* That's a very vulnerable place for a staff member potentially.

Respect for People Has to Do with Treating People Well but, More Importantly, with Maximizing Human Potential

When Virginia Mason board member Carolyn Corvi started at Boeing she traveled to a Toyota plant in Lexington, Kentucky, to learn and try to understand what defines the Toyota culture. She says:

> It was clear to me then that it was about people and how people were treated. The Toyota leaders always start by talking about people: 'How do we work with one another? How do we respect one another?' Respect for people has to do with treating people well, but more importantly, it means maximizing human potential. The founders of the Toyota Production System believed that people are the only source for innovative ideas, so the philosophy of developing people's potential becomes essential.

In a way it was perfectly natural for leaders at Virginia Mason not to tackle respect for people at the outset. It may well have constituted overload. They were going through a hugely disruptive period of change—learning an entirely new management method—and another straw on the camel's back might have been too much. Leaders believed early on that they needed to learn the methodology and the tools, to become proficient at it, and to spread it throughout the organization.

"As the management system matured," says Corvi, "I believe the leaders learned that the on-going development of people was at the heart of continuous improvement. It is disrespectful to expect people to work in a system that produces waste. When people are encouraged to use their brains to eliminate waste, they are respected. I believe this is the natural evolution of the system."

Respect for People Makes Lean Management Work

Bob Emiliani is a lean management guru with a voluminous output of books and articles. A number of Virginia Mason executives have learned from his work and from a presentation he made while visiting Virginia Mason. Emiliani has a particular expertise in the Respect for People aspect of the Toyota Production System, and in a 2009 paper he observed that "Lean community leaders have recently made two huge changes in how they present Lean. The first change is Lean as a management system rather than 'lean manufacturing.' Second, they are finally taking note of the long-established Respect for People principle," which, as Emiliani puts it, has been "hiding in plain view for decades."

Emiliani notes that while continuous improvement is the better known of the "two pillars of The Toyota Way," the other pillar is Respect for People, and he offers an elucidating quick tour of the origins and evolution of the "Respect for People" principle in his paper.

> Top managers typically possess superficial, casual definitions of "Respect for People" such as fairness, civility, or listening. And they think they do these things quite well. Further, they think understanding the meaning of "Respect for People" is trivial for well-educated persons in high positions. This is a severe misjudgment. Far from being trivial, it is of great importance to the long-term survival and prosperity of a business to understand what "Respect for People" really means…
>
> Toyota's top-level representation of the "Respect for People" principle consists of two parts: "Respect" and "Teamwork…'
>
> RESPECT: We respect others, make every effort to understand each other, take responsibility and do our best to build mutual trust.
>
> TEAMWORK: We stimulate personal and professional growth, share the opportunities of development and maximize individual and team performance." [Copyright 2009 Bob Emiliani; "The Equally Important 'Respect for People' Principle" by Bob Emiliani; www.bobemiliani.com]

Emiliani observes that the Respect for People principle encompasses all key stakeholders: employees, suppliers, customers, investors, and communities. His paper is particularly enlightening when he highlights thoughts from a variety of Toyota Production System experts. Toyota chair Fujio Cho wrote that when workers are respected they "are allowed to display in full their capabilities through active participation in running and improving their own workshops…" And when they do so workers are able to "fully [display] their capabilities," creating a rich environment of respect. [Co-authored 1977 paper]

Sensei Kato keenly observed the connection between leadership and respect for people in his memoir *My Years With Toyota* (1981): "Handing down orders is not leadership, nor is issuing policies enough to constitute business relationships. In my view leadership is a process springing from dialogue that reaches the level of true communication, followed by sincere efforts at cooperation based upon mutual consideration and understanding of each other's position." It is often perceived that the soul of the Toyota Production System is a relentless effort to eliminate waste, yet former Toyota executive Taiichi Ohno wrote that "respect for humanity" is "equally important" [Toyota Production System: Beyond Large-Scale Production (1988)]

Michael Husar, an executive at a General Motors-Toyota joint venture, wrote that "mutual trust means that management and the employees have confidence in one another... Mutual trust comes from the belief that everyone is...striving for the same purpose... Toyota realizes this kind of mutual trust is not a given condition between management and the employees. It must be earned through many mutual efforts that create confidence." [Memo entitled "Corporate Culture: Toyota's Secret, Competitive Advantage." 1991] This notion that alignment promotes mutual trust is essential not only to Toyota but also to Virginia Mason.

A Substantial Barrier to Progress in Patient Safety Is a Dysfunctional Culture Rooted in Widespread Disrespect

A greater emphasis on respect for people had evolved over time at Virginia Mason. Throughout the financial crisis, for example, when virtually every other provider organization in the Seattle area was experiencing layoffs, Virginia Mason had none. And employees continued to receive bonuses during that challenging financial period. Nonetheless, for the greater part of the Virginia Mason journey the focus had been largely on the management method and its tools. The feedback from employees after the service training broadened leadership's focus to include a greater emphasis on Respect for People.

After a number of discussions, executives decided to reach out for guidance from Dr. Lucian Leape, an expert on safety and respect in health care. Leape is a Boston surgeon and leader of the Lucian Leape Institute at the National Patient Safety Foundation.

A number of the leaders at Virginia Mason were familiar with Leape and his work. Cathie Furman suggested inviting Leape to come to Virginia Mason to help guide the leaders. In May 2011, Leape traveled to Seattle for two and a half days of work. "Lucian has got all the credentials so doctors will listen to him," says Furman. "*Everybody* listens to him."

At the core of Leape's message is the theme enunciated for some years now by Paul O'Neill, the former U.S. secretary of the treasury and Alcoa chief executive officer. O'Neill says that respect in the workplace exists when employees can confidently state that the following three statements are accurate:

- Can I say every day I am treated with dignity and respect by everyone I encounter without respect to my pay grade, or my title, or my race, or etchnicity or religious beliefs or gender?
- Am I given the things I need—education, training, tools and encouragement—to develop my full potential so I can make a contribution to the organization that gives meaning to my life?
- Am I recognized and appreciated for the work I do?

Being able to say yes to all three of these provides "joy and meaning in work," says Leape. Speaking to Virginia Mason leaders, he noted that the spectrum of disrespectful behavior goes beyond the obvious (e.g., tantrums, dressing down staff members) to a toxic "passive disrespect" where, for example, clinicians knowingly fail to follow standard work. The "spectrum of disrespectful behavior," he said includes disruptive behavior, humiliation, and degrading putdowns.

Leape emphasized several points from his articles in *Academic Medicine*, where he argued that "a substantial barrier to progress in patient safety is a dysfunctional culture rooted in widespread disrespect. Disrespect is a threat to patient safety because it inhibits collegiality and co-operation essential to teamwork, cuts off communication, undermines morale, and inhibits compliance with and implementation of new practices."

But leaders can strengthen a culture of safety by becoming role models who always treat colleagues—regardless of their position—with the utmost respect. Leape echoed Bob Emiliani in saying that leaders need to do a better job of understanding the true nature and power of respect for people; that is, it is not civility and politeness but rather a richer notion that enables open and honest communication and facilitates the difficult discussion for the sake of improved communication as well as patient and staff safety.

Foundational Behaviors of Respect for People

One of Virginia Mason's signature achievements was the development of its Patient Safety Alert (PSA) system. It was derived from observing Toyota workers and their leaders intervene on the factory floor to prevent a defect from being passed down the line. Every Virginia Mason employee was empowered to stop the line as Toyota workers did in Japan and to report a safety alert if they believed there was potential for patient harm. While every worker was empowered to call a PSA the question was whether every employee was comfortable doing so. Unsurprisingly, the answer was no.

Introducing the notion to American health care that every employee is empowered to monitor anything and everything they observe presents jarring cultural challenges. Too many workers were reluctant to file a PSA, considering it somehow punitive against another employee or department. Some employees believed that the PSA system failed to clearly distinguish between error and misconduct. The notion that it was not about blame but about safety had not fully penetrated the organization.

The issue of respect was a key element holding back the PSA system. Leape emphasized that a culture of safety rests upon a foundation of open, honest discussion among all staff members. When there is a fear of speaking up the culture is poisoned and patients are at risk. Chafetz considered Leape's visit and the themes he enunciated to be nothing less than a "seminal moment in our journey. His focus is around the whole concept of disruptive behavior, respect for people but not just the *obvious*—surgeons throwing instruments across the room. He focuses on the disrespect that's more covert. That's really important to the work that we're doing."

After the Leape visit, Chafetz, along with Susan Haufe, administrative director of patient relations and service, and her team led an organization-wide effort to solicit opinions from *all* workers focused on defining "how we treat each other." Surveys asked employees what respect looks like and received hundreds of responses in just a few days. Building upon the feedback, Chafetz and her colleagues convened a large advisory team with representatives from across the organization. Virginia Mason leaders went to the troops, inviting feedback on the internal intranet site and hosting a series of focus groups where employees spoke their minds. Employees and leaders identified 10 foundational behaviors of respect:

1. **Listen to understand.** Good listening means giving the speaker your full attention. Nonverbal cues like eye contact and nodding let others know you are paying attention and are fully present for the conversation. Avoid interrupting or cutting others off when they are speaking.
2. **Keep your promises.** When you keep your word you show you are honest and you let others know you value them. Follow through on commitments and if you run into problems, let others know. Be reliable and expect reliability from others.
3. **Be encouraging.** Giving encouragement shows you care about others and their success. It is essential that everyone at Virginia Mason understand his or her contributions have value. Encourage your coworkers to share their ideas, opinions, and perspectives.
4. **Connect with others.** Notice those around you and smile. This acknowledgment, combined with a few sincere words of greeting, creates a powerful connection. Practice courtesy and kindness in all interactions.
5. **Express gratitude.** A heartfelt thank you can often make a person's day and shows you notice and appreciate their work. Use the Virginia Mason applause system (an internal recognition program), a handwritten note, verbal praise, or share a story of going above and beyond at your next team meeting.

6. **Share information.** When people know what is going on, they feel valued and included. Be sure everyone has the information he or she needs to do his or her work and knows about things that affect his or her work environment. Sharing information and communicating openly signals you trust and respect others.

7. **Speak up.** It is our responsibility to ensure a safe environment for everyone at Virginia Mason—not just physical safety but also mental and emotional safety. Create an environment where we all feel comfortable to speak up if we see something unsafe or feel unsafe.

8. **Walk in their shoes.** Empathize with others; understand their point of view and their contributions. Be considerate of their time, job responsibilities, and workload. Ask before you assume your priorities are their priorities.

9. **Grow and develop.** Value your own potential by committing to continuous learning. Take advantage of opportunities to gain knowledge and learn new skills. Share your knowledge and expertise with others. Ask for and be open to feedback to grow both personally and professionally.

10. **Be a team player.** Great teams are great because team members support each other. Create a work environment where help is happily offered, asked for, and received. Trust that teammates have good intentions. Anticipate other team members' needs, and clearly communicate priorities and expectations to be sure the workload is level loaded.

Summarizing these elements and the plan to instill them in the culture, Chafetz addressed a group of leaders and connected respect to the Strategic Plan. She said, "Respect for people will help us strengthen the environment to achieve our vision of being the quality leader and transforming health care. And it supports all of our pillars—people, quality, service, and innovation—and provides us with tools for continuous learning, leadership, and team commitments to behaviors that enable us to deliver the perfect patient experience." She noted that Respect for People had been an overall organizational goal at Virginia Mason throughout 2012 and would continue into 2013. "We tend to sort goals into quality or service or innovation, and this was the first goal that explicitly crossed all the pillars of our Strategic Plan," she says. "This influences our culture, the way we do our work, our patients—everything."

The link between respect and VMPS was clear. "We expect our people to engage in safe, respectful behavior and understand patient safety, but we don't deliberately and consistently teach the fundamentals and behaviors to support that expectation," she says. "Health care workers have not traditionally been taught this. This is changing, but there's an urgency to change for the sake of our patients and staff." As leaders, she said it was important to "break the cycle" to change behavior in the future. "This means leader accountability to coach and role model is more important than ever. We have to model very specific behaviors that support a culture of respect."

Leadership development to help coach and model respectful behavior drew Virginia Mason executives to the Open School at the Institute for Healthcare Improvement, where the IHI Patient Safety Curriculum proved valuable. Drawn from a variety of experts on safety in health care, the online guidance is clear and quickly applicable. A key part of learning was training leaders to understand, model, and coach behaviors that support a culture of safety. Leaders may think they are already doing precisely that but training helps clarify and sharpen these skills.

Virginia Mason teams found value in a program developed by the U.S. Department of Defense in cooperation with the federal Agency for Healthcare Research and Quality. The program, called TeamSTEPPS, is essentially a program that emphasizes teamwork and communication to improve safety in a health care environment. The program helps to clarify roles and responsibilities of team members, which improves accountability and communication.

Theater as Training

Virginia Mason leaders approached Respect for People training in an unusual manner. Rather than telling employees about positive and negative behaviors, leaders hired professional actors to *show* them. In one scene, a supervisor arrives at a meeting with three of her direct reports. The staffers are seated around a table and clearly expecting the supervisor to join them. But she remains aloof, standing apart from them issuing orders. Her tone is barely professional, lacking even a hint of warmth or engagement. She is neither guiding nor coaching her employees. She is dismissive of their questions and skeptical of their suggestions. The employees are clearly deflated by this. It is a dramatic example of daily work-place disrespect. She never insults anyone or raises her voice or acts out. All of her actions, however, scream disrespect.

Another scene showed two staff members at the end of the workday feeling discouraged. And then the actors dug into what had occurred during the day to get the employees feeling down— for example, a series of subtle putdowns and being ignored, which are the nearly invisible and unintentional slights so common in a health care setting. The actors deftly showed what happened to create those emotions and showed the impact of those behaviors. Many members of the audiences found this quite powerful and affecting.

The play was both entertaining and intense. The scenes were drawn from real-life experiences at Virginia Mason, and the tension in a number of scenes where people were treated disrespectfully was uncomfortable. The play was staged 21 times over a period of weeks to enable all employees on all shifts to see it. In fact, Virginia Mason leaders felt this training was so crucial that attendance at the play was mandatory. A key focus was to understand that there is obvious disruptive behavior and also passive disrespect that is subtler and just as unacceptable. "It was very effective at showing scenes where people were feeling disrespected while other scenes showed what it was like to have great teamwork and respect," says Chafetz.

After each showing of the play a Virginia Mason executive would facilitate a discussion with the audience concerning what they had found most instructive. Dr. Bob Caplan facilitated discussions after two different showings of the play, and he found the experience enriching. One aspect of the training that Caplan thought particularly important was that it was done with "a mixed-employee model. It was not all docs then all nurses. The training involved cross-sections of the organization and that was important. These fundamental behaviors apply to everyone and we practiced the concepts together. It was one of the first times we had ever trained as a full organization." Caplan concluded:

> On one occasion, the performance took place in Kirkland, a suburb of Seattle, in a small community theater that seated about 150 people. This was an opportunity to do the training for staff members from four of our neighborhood clinics, a group composed mostly of primary care providers and primary care staff. The feeling inside of this theater is intimate: the stage is tucked right into the seating area, and the curve of the theater creates good eye contact not only with those on the stage but also among those in audience. This was an opportunity for staff to really "see" each other and their responses.
>
> When it was about 15 minutes before the performance, I went into the theater and talked to folks as they sat down. I specifically asked a few people that I knew if I could call on them during the discussion portion of the program.
>
> When it was time for the audience to participate and share their personal reactions and their action plans, I started by asking for one of my colleagues in the audience to be the first. This was a well-known, well-respected, and very warm-hearted primary care physician. That's all it took to break the ice and turn on the engagement. From that point onward, comments came from nurses, medical assistants, and support staff. The compelling performance by the actors and the eye contact afforded by the small theater promoted a group conversation. The audience was not so much responding to my questions, "What opportunity do you see? What is your personal action plan?" as they were talking to each other about what they were connecting to and understanding. On this occasion, I thought the lasting power of this training came from the fact that the participants were making a commitment with each other—and these commitments were forming on the spot.

After the play, leaders at all levels worked in small groups with their teams to discuss the lessons they had learned and to practice the 10 respectful behaviors. During the course of training for respectful behaviors, Virginia Mason team members were asked to select two of the top 10 behaviors to focus on, and the top two chosen were *listen to understand* and *speak up*.

The theater piece was especially powerful for *showing* staffers important behaviors. "It demonstrated that we respected staff members enough not to just send them an email or brochure but also to bring them to a presentation where the organization's values are dramatized in that way," says Susan Haufe. "It really engaged the team. People enjoyed it. The actors did a great job coming up with realistic scenarios—stuff you see going on all the time where you've done it yourself or seen it happening to others."

I Have a Concern

Kathy Shingleton, director of human resources, recalls one physician who was reluctant to engage with the training program. "He said he didn't want to go because there was nothing he could learn," she recalls. "But after he completed the training he said, 'I never realized about the passive disrespect that was occurring in the OR until I went to Respect for People.' Because of his position and his *power* in the OR, he didn't *mean* to be disrespectful, but he was being *perceived* to be disrespectful and he had no awareness of the perception."

Central to the training was listening carefully for certain language. For example, now, when a Virginia Mason staff member says to another, "I have a concern," ears perk up and people listen attentively, for this is the precise language that signals a possible safety concern. The initials CUS have taken on real meaning: I am **C**oncerned. I am **U**ncomfortable. This is a **S**afety issue (or I don't feel like this is **S**afe).

"Respect for People has rapidly become integrated into our culture," says Chapman. "It's not dissimilar to the patient. We always ask, 'Is that patient first? Is that patient focused?' Now the word *respect* has a very similar power. 'Is that respectful?' If you don't have respect for each other, then a nurse will never be able to call a doctor on something she sees as unsafe. She'll never be emboldened or empowered to speak up. That really got hammered home."

Dr. Catherine Potts, chief of primary care, says she sees a greater willingness among staff members to speak up when they perceive something might be off kilter. "People now realize that they can speak up freely without fear of retribution; that there will not be anything like a shaming event." Tachibana shares that view. "It certainly affects psychological safety," she says. "When you create a culture where people can feel safe to say what needs to be said, to be transparent, to call out issues, to bring forth problems, to challenge peoples' thinking in respectful ways that have the best interest of the patient at heart, it means they do not have to make a difficult decision about whether they are going to be *safe* to do what they know or say what they know needs to be said."

This marked improvement in psychological safety that Tachibana perceives has had a powerful impact on actual patient safety as well, says Furman. Since the Respect for People training, she has measured a "huge spike in patient safety alerts."

We Are All in the Same Value Stream

Respect for People has clearly improved safety at Virginia Mason, and if it had accomplished nothing else that improvement would still be an enormous achievement. But the respect effort has done much more than that: it has strengthened the management method that is at the core of Virginia Mason. Across the board Virginia Mason leaders believe that Respect for People strengthens the Virginia Mason Production System. Dr. Michael Glenn, chief medical officer, says there is real power when he and his medical assistant and other team members get together "and we all publicly put orange dots on what we're going to work on and then we follow-up with each other at meetings. It takes it away from a power-based approach. Do it because I'm your boss versus to do it because it's best for the patients and we need to work as a team and we need to be respectful to each other to be successful in doing that. And we are all working across value streams and when you do that you actually realize that *we are all in the same value stream* and everyone is your teammate and we are aligned with our focus on the patient."

"I *love* the fact that *my* colleagues focus on the Respect for People behaviors," says Chapman. "I don't sense that I've got colleagues thinking, 'I'm not going to do that or that doesn't make sense in my part of the organization.' We agree and even those that don't agree initially, they still commit. And I love that. I don't feel like I'm kind of fighting the tide the other way."

There are hundreds, perhaps thousands, of tangible examples of the improvement in respectful behavior throughout the medical center and its clinics—in all departments. Perhaps one of the more interesting involves those invisible workers who toil in the depths of the hospital within sterile processing. Denise Dubuque passionately pursues work that is based on respecting the sterile processing team. In practice, this means reducing the massive waste of 60–70 percent of sterilized surgical equipment never being used and being shipped back down to the team to clean and sterilize once again. If there is a classic definition of waste in the Toyota Production System, this may be it.

The idea that Dubuque and her colleagues are working on is called Build to Order—constructing pans of surgical instruments tailored to both the procedure and the surgeon doing the work. Different procedures require different instruments, of course, and different surgeons vary in their preferences in the OR. "We are going to give each surgeon a customized set of instruments for what they use," says Dubuque.

This has taken and will continue to take a significant amount of study and analysis, but she is convinced they will soon get there. "We believe that the Build to Order initiative is about Respect for People," she says. "I have passion to come to work every day as a leader, saying, 'How can I help this team be successful?' Because every day that goes on that we're not getting to that goal of Build to Order we're disrespecting the team."

What Does Leadership Look Like?

If there is one essential key to the success of Virginia Mason's Respect for People it is that leaders throughout the organization model the behavior and work closely with their teams coaching and guiding. Says Patterson:

That is how you make it happen. That is how you have to execute. It's about having leaders right there side by side with our employees. It is the respect for people and how we treat each other but it's so much deeper than that. It's this: As a leader, do I give you the opportunity to identify the problems we need to fix and then work right there fixing them? It isn't leaders deciding. It's the people who do the work. They know what's important to the organization. But I think that the key is that as leaders, as we're doing our work, the behaviors we exhibit out on the genba must always be respectful.

There is a world of difference between being out on the genba creating fear and blaming people and accusing them of not doing something versus truly modeling transparency. Critical to this is how do you leverage every single person that works in the company, not just say, "Hey, come to work and clock in and clock out." We need people to come to work and make a difference.

Sometimes we see people that are disengaged. They come to work but they're not really engaged. I think we're upping the bar for all our staff members and so when I talk about respect for people, I say, "We respect people and part of that is having high expectations that they're going to be part of our work." When I go to our new employee orientation, I say, "I hope somebody mentioned along your interview process that we have high expectations that you're going to help us transform health care because it's a two-way deal."

Chapter 5

We Are a Leadership Team, not a Compilation of Leaders

A Team Journey

The Virginia Mason leadership team was formed 4800 miles from the medical center campus on Seattle's First Hill. In 2002, when Dr. Gary Kaplan led his executive team to Japan for immersion in the study and practice of the Toyota Production System, there was one of those defining moments, when those present recall it years later as though it happened yesterday. The moment occurred in a conference room after the group had been in Japan for 14 days. This group had been through a grueling experience for more than a year. They all had major responsibilities within the organization, but for more than 12 months they had also all been involved in a deep dive into the methods and tools of the Toyota Production System. They had read thousands of pages from books and articles. They had visited lean manufacturing companies in Seattle and Hartford. And now they had completed an exhausting period of work, study, and observation in a factory. A moment that would be seen in retrospect as one of the most pivotal in the 94-year history of Virginia Mason was upon them.

The session came the night before the team's scheduled departure for the United States. Kaplan asked each person around the table—34 in all—to share whatever thoughts they had: honest, unvarnished thoughts about whether adapting the Toyota Production System to health care was the right pathway forward. Kaplan made it clear that he was committed to this direction. "And if you didn't agree, that was okay," recalls Dr. Donna Smith. "But you had to speak. We needed to talk about this. It wasn't a given that we would have consensus... The idea was, *'We've got to figure this out together.'* We were pushing each other's thinking, challenging each other to make sure we were making the right decision."

In the course of the trip there had been a perceptible shift. The team had done the reading and study and observed lean methods in the United States, but now they had seen the method and tools practiced to a high art form. "During the first half of the trip we could not say wholeheartedly that we knew where we were headed with this," recalls Diane Miller. "But there were dinners and discussions, and all of that time we spent talking about the implication this had for health care enabled us to reach a point at the end of the trip where we agreed that this would be our management method." Perhaps it was a mix of the intensity of the trip as well as the immensity of the challenge they were about to undertake. They were pioneers with all the excitement, promise, and peril that entailed. No one in health care had ever before attempted what they were about to do. This was as uncharted as territory could get in twenty-first-century health care management. The stakes could hardly have been higher. A decision to embrace the Toyota method was fraught with risks—calculated risks, but risks, nonetheless.

The conference room gathering on the eve of the return home was a moment of deep bonding among the men and women on that team, for, at least in part, the session was tinged by a sense of loss, even grief. Yes, there was exhilaration at the possibility of what lay ahead. But there was also the sense among a number of team members that they had been working so very hard in a system that was about to be abandoned—tossed aside in favor of a radically new way of doing business. Had they labored hard for so long in a flawed system? With flawed methods and tools? Had the system they'd operated in been inadequate? And the inescapable conclusion was that yes, it was inadequate, that there was—they now believed—a better way. "We were so moved by the power of this that on the last day there were a lot of tears," recalls Miller. "People that I would have never pictured crying were quite moved by it."

Of the 34-team members on the 2002 Japan trip, 19 remain in leadership roles at Virginia Mason 12 years later. Longevity matters in the stability of the organization and in its ability to build and sustain a particular culture. It matters in the organization's knowledge base related to the Toyota methods. And it matters when it comes to glue that binds the team: trust. Says Dr. Robert Caplan, medical director of quality, "We are a leadership team, not a compilation of leaders." And Charleen Tachibana observed, "There is a commitment here to long-term careers and to long-term development of talent. Look at our colleagues in the Pacific Northwest. A chief nursing officer turns about every three years. There is very little anybody can do in an executive team that turns every three years. These are long term strategies and if you turn every three years that's very short-term. You need a long-term commitment and willingness to work with individuals to develop talent over time for the benefit of the organization."

The Gold Is in the Work of the Team, not Superstars

The Virginia Mason Production System both depends on and builds strong teams. During a kaizen event such as a Rapid Process Improvement Workshop, relationships among team members strengthen. Siloes come down and hierarchical walls are broken through. People get to understand one another's work, get to walk in each other's shoes. "VMPS is totally team based," says Dr. Joyce Lammert. "When we do RPIWs and kaizen events, it really teaches people how to be a team every time you do it. And it's the only way we get our work done, so you have to rely on people and have trust in people." Says Tachibana, "The gold is in the work of the team and the synergies of the team members not relying on superstars."

The dyad structure of leadership is pivotal at Virginia Mason for it pairs administrative and clinical leaders at the top of every department. Kaplan believes strongly in the dyad leadership approach in which a physician and administrator are paired together to lead a department. "The dyad characterizes our leadership structure in all clinical areas. Leadership is lonely so a partnership is an important enabler of strong leadership. Many physicians have major trust issues with hierarchical authority. By having physician–administrator teams, you can leverage different but complementary skill sets and identify with the clinical care world much more closely. Sometimes the physician is in front, sometimes the administrator is in front, but we speak with one voice."

Quickly forming teams as situations warrant enables staff members at all levels to work with a wide variety of colleagues throughout the medical center helping people develop and strengthen many different relationships.

This "boundary hopping," as Tachibana calls it, helps people "understand the greater good of the organization so that you're not in an advocacy role advocating for just your department. And because it's not advocacy leadership there's this greater sense of team that probably goes beyond what most organizations experience as team." Boundary hopping is possible at Virginia Mason because the organization is not dependent on leaders with a particular area of clinical or technical expertise—very much unlike most health care organizations. Says Lynne Chafetz:

> We are more focused on leadership competency versus individual technical skills. You can learn new subject matter but you have to have leadership competencies to lead the team. As an example, I was involved with a 3P (Production, Preparation, Process) on optimizing care transitions, and I was on the guiding team for that organizational goal for a couple years. It was really focused on how we communicate effectively with our patients who have congestive heart failure. What information do they need to be successful as they leave the hospital? How do we have an effective hand-off to the primary care doctor?
>
> The idea that [as chief counsel] I would have an opportunity to do that work here and provide some leadership of a workshop is

an important component of our management method in the sense that I'm trained in the management method to be able to lead a workshop. It doesn't really matter what the *content* is. I know what I need to do to go out and get the data, and I know what I need to do to set the targets and it's not just me. It's the team.

Throughout the years the team has worked to break down siloes. Essential to doing so is identifying and focusing on cross-organizational goals that the entire team agrees to focus on. "We've backed it up with our compensation," says Sue Anderson. "Part of my bonus depends on how well we do with glycemic control in the hospital. It allows us as a peer group to move in the same direction."

Bonus payments in health care can be controversial. At Virginia Mason the bonus payments to senior executives are dependent not on how a particular individual, group, or department performs but on how the *organization as a whole* performs on that year's targeted goals, which are established by the executive team and approved by the health system board of directors. "Some goals are initiatives that have been identified by individual executives; others are continuing from prior years," says Chafetz. "It is not that different areas of the organization pursue their own goals apart from the whole. It is not that the hospital goes off and does their stuff or the clinic goes off and does their stuff. It's the whole executive senior leadership team coming together and spending a fair amount of time going through every organizational priority and organizational goal."

A deep understanding of the Toyota methods and tools is fundamental to being able to achieve any of the overall goals. Says Caplan:

We set a bar for everyone having a certain degree of competency in lean. All managers must have lean certification and we all train together. The expectation is that we are all learning and growing together. It is a very powerful accelerant when we move ahead not like we are dragging leaders behind us—but together as leaders. This is strengthened by our concept of standard work for leaders. As leaders, we hold each other accountable for leading in a standardized way. Our leadership training is about all of us. Success depends on all of us being on the same page and getting to the next page at the same time. For the organization that has a very powerful effect. When we grow and evolve as leaders the organization sees consistent growth. When we all lead the same way it lowers anxiety and confusion in the organization.

An example of learning together is the work being done to improve the patient experience of care. Led by Dr. Donna Smith, patient experience physician executive, it is central to overall improvement within the organization:

> We have learned a lot about what it takes for people to realize what a difference they can make in a patient's experience. The lesson is that *everyone matters*. The physicians increased their engagement and interest when we developed tools and support to help improvement. Initially, we just reported scores without offering an improvement pathway, but since we started courses and coaching, engagement among physicians and staff has increased. Mandatory training for everyone together—that is, all team members taking the same class, practicing together—has also helped. This included basic service training, training about empathy, and most recently our organization-wide respect for people curriculum.

The Essential Nature of Trust

When speaking with leaders at Virginia Mason, it is common to hear of their desire for vulnerability. "To create an environment of trust where your team members feel comfortable and safe speaking up, you have to make yourself vulnerable as a leader to be empathetic," says Chafetz. "It cannot be that the leader's attitude is, 'I'm up here and everything's great.' You have to be willing to talk about your failures and humanize yourself as a leader to create that foundation of trust." Says Steve Schaefer, "We try to be as vulnerable as possible because when we are vulnerable we trust each other and trust leads to speed and speed leads to transformation."

Over time, trust and alignment imbue the team with courage. "You don't have to be courageous in the heroic sense," says Lammert, "if you've got a strong team that's aligned." In part, trust is derived from shared values such as all leaders being on the genba engaging with staff, patients, visitors—everyone. Says Chapman:

> It does not matter what your leadership or management title is you're expected to stop and engage a patient and help them to their destination. If you see garbage on the ground, you pick it up. And I love the fact that at Virginia Mason that truly happens. It's not just, "Oh, I'll let the staff do that and I can just go on by because I've got a meeting." I love the fact that my colleagues are so committed to the Respect for People behaviors, the Walking in Their Shoes, the Listening to Understand, sharing information—when we go through a development program like that we're all in.

Chapman pinpoints a vital difference between Virginia Mason and many other organizations:

> I don't sense that I've got colleagues that have the attitude, "Ah, I'm not going to do that," or, "That doesn't make sense in my part of the organization." In organizations where that happens, you have to articulate to your team why another team doesn't have to adhere to certain standards but your team does because this leadership component agrees and this one doesn't. That just doesn't happen here.

Jim Cote, senior vice president and clinic administrator, has worked at a number of provider organizations, and he sees a greater level of trust among team members at Virginia Mason than at previous places he has worked. "There is trust among everyone on the team," he observes. "As opposed to previous places I've been where if I am not at this meeting I know my point of view will not be represented."

Most of the Leaders Here Are Intrinsically Motivated

While the power and effectiveness of the team derives from alignment around the Virginia Mason Production System, the team culture goes deeper than the management method, deeper than common language and goals. The nucleus that binds and drives the team is a desire to improve the lives of the patients and communities they serve—and to change health care for everyone. "I think most of the leaders here are intrinsically motivated," says Dr. Lammert. "They're values-driven. I talk to lots of lawyers who have been patients of mine and people from large corporations, and it doesn't seem that all that many of these people are all that happy. And *we have something that gives meaning to what we do every day.* Listening to somebody and being privy to the important things in his or her life—*what a gift.* It is the opportunity and ability to comfort and heal and guide."

Tachibana says that for most members of the leadership team the mission is about values:

> We have aligned people's beliefs with those of the organization. People have passion about their work. Their job is a personal mission to make a difference, to change things for the better. Some people internally describe it as a moral imperative. I can't *not* do this. There is a synergy there that ignites the connection between clarity of values of the organization connected to people's personal values.
>
> The merging of personal and organizational values is a powerful energy source driving the leadership team. How do you just say, "We're not going to do that"? The team talks about a moral imperative to do this work because I don't know how you actually realize the potential and then choose *not* to. Why do you really do what you do? What's the greater cause you're trying to impact and affect here? That creates personal urgency.
>
> For me, leadership here is a vocation, and I think it that's true for many of us. It's a calling here. It's a vocation and it's such a gift to do it with others who are in vocations with you and want to travel there with you. For me it's a very spiritual journey here. I can't imagine doing it elsewhere because of the risk of losing that component. But I would say leadership here, for most people, is a vocation. It's a calling.

Tachibana recalled an executive meeting to review organizational goals, and someone asked a pointed question: *Is it too much?* Were they overreaching? What if they did not achieve all of their stated goals? She said:

> My perspective has always been that I would *not* expect to achieve everything we put on our goals because if you achieve it, how do

you know what greater capacity we had? You have to be able to fail or to not achieve some of it to understand where you have optimally challenged your team to go as far as they can go.

You have to be careful so you don't implode everybody, but to say that you hit everything, every year would have to make you ask, "Are we pushing hard enough? Are we doing it smart enough? Why is it that we can hit everything?" The targets aren't strong enough or high enough or you haven't stretched yourself enough to do it.

Julie Morath joined the Virginia Mason board in January 2009. From the start, she observed the intrinsic motivation that Lammert and Tachibana describe:

There is alignment, but it is not a transactional business model alignment. It is alignment to fidelity of purpose and to deep respect for people. There is real clarity of vision and purpose. It's a highly relational alignment based on common purpose and constancy of purpose—a real passion around that. It is different from a lot of places where alignment works because of incentives. This has a little higher order to it—higher order because people give discretionary energy. They're not just doing the job. There is always this sense of inquiry—getting better as a way of life. When we look at the triple aim and hospitals under siege we know patients and families deserve more, society deserves more than we have been delivering in terms of value.

The intrinsic motivation is personal desire and organizational commitment to make the world a better place by improving health care. "We talk about that being our north star—patient at the top—a deep commitment fueled by knowing we can do something about it," says Dr. Smith.

It Is the Egalitarian Sense that Every Team Member Has Something Valuable to Add

"Our success as a team depends on all of us being on the same page and getting to the next page at the same time," says Caplan. "We are not just aligned. We are growing together and we challenge one another together. We hold one another accountable, and we do it with a sense of urgency and mission." Caplan notes that keeping one another accountable requires courageous conversations that can be uncomfortable. Mike Ondracek, vice president of clinic operations, has experience at other major health care organizations in the northwest. He observes:

> There are conversations that take place at Virginia Mason that typically don't take place in other organizations. When individual situations arise that are not consistent with expectations, leaders will take that moment to share directly how and why the specific interaction did not achieve the desired results. Providing immediate feedback ensures that we are respecting each other. It's disrespectful *not* to say anything. Respectful timely feedback is part of our culture at Virginia Mason.

When Kathy Shingleton arrived at Virginia Mason as head of human resources after 25 years at other organizations, she was surprised by the requirements for Virginia Mason leaders:

> There is nowhere else in America where that kind of training is a pre-requisite for leaders. It's one thing to get through the training but we require people to exhibit the skills. We require that throughout their time here. No one else does that. And we require standard work for leaders. No one else does that. We require that for the whole house. No one else does that.
>
> We require leaders to lead events and to present in front of their peers and to lead multilevel teams. That's a requirement to lead here. You can't lead here if you don't do that, and we also require that of physician leaders. We treat physician leaders the same way we treat administrative leaders. No one else does that because usually there's a dichotomy. We treat physician leaders here and administrative leaders the same. I don't know anybody that does that. Most people in health care still have physicians on a pedestal.

The team approach sets Virginia Mason apart from many other hierarchical health care organizations, places where challenging the hierarchy is discouraged. These hierarchies, commonly built within siloed medical departments, tend to calcify over time. The inward-looking nature of men and women within these siloes can sometimes make for wonderful patient care in specific areas, but it subverts the notion of providing a great patient experience across the continuum of care.

Denise Dubuque has worked at other health care organizations, and her view is that the other places are much less team oriented than Virginia Mason. "There is no question there is a difference at Virginia Mason," she says. "No question. It is the egalitarian sense that every team member has something valuable to add. At Virginia Mason that is for real. It's for real and it is truly the DNA of the organization." Says Smith, "Involving others in improvement work helps them see themselves in the story so that no matter where you are—whether it is the front desk or wherever—you can see yourself in the patient experience through their care. As front desk person, you can see yourself as part of the bigger picture here, that you are the critical first touch for person as they arrive in the hospital sick and scared."

Siloes and hierarchy are inimical to patient safety. Dubuque says that in a practical sense—under the pressure of the OR, for example—the Virginia Mason approach can make for better, safer care than other organizations that tend to be hierarchical and siloed.

There are very tense situations in an operating room environment, so it is not uncommon for team members including surgeons to be under stress and to speak firmly to their team members. At times there is disrespectful language. And that creates a culture of timidity and fear, a culture where staff members may be reluctant to speak up when they think something may be going wrong. In one case a physician rebuked a nurse when she pointed out—correctly—the protocol that should have been followed before providing certain medication to a patient. When the nurse pushed back to prevent harm to the patient, the physicians turned nasty and belittled her. When the nurse called in a patient safety alert, the medical department leadership came to the nurse's defense and required that the physician apologize to the nurse and that he enter an anger management class.

"I worry that there aren't as many people working on this issue of respect," says Dubuque. "I worry how other organizations respond to medical errors and just accept the fact that, 'Oh, these things happen sometimes and that's just part of doing business.' Or they don't have a culture in which there really has been that alignment with the leadership structure where if I stand up for a staff member with a provider and that provider doesn't like it I know I have backup. I know that the leadership team is supportive of me."

Chapter 6

Identifying Talent, Developing Leaders

"It is incumbent on us to have the very best leaders," says CEO Dr. Gary Kaplan. "I have told my team I want all 'A' players in every key leadership position or people with the potential to become 'A' players. There is a whole cohort in health care where there are leaders who are not 'A' players and do not have the potential to become 'A' players. But I insist on it because we must deliver on behalf of our patients and our community."

What does this mean in reality? How are strong leaders identified and developed at Virginia Mason? In this chapter we explore the organization's leadership selection and development process first by describing various initiatives that strengthen leadership development and then by detailing the experiences of five executives whose paths to leadership convey important lessons.

* * *

"One of our most important jobs as leaders is to ensure development of talent and leaders for succession planning, the next generation," says Kaplan. "We are very planful about that." That planful nature includes intensive and ongoing talent reviews, executive coaching, individual development planning, mentoring programs and resources, special and rotation assignments, and external leader development programs. These various initiatives are guided by a series of overriding principles. The first is that "talent is owned at the organizational level," says Kathy Shingleton, vice president of human resources. "We are different from other organizations in this respect. We move people around throughout the organization to develop talent. We do not silo people—keeping clinical people in the clinical realm and business people in the business realm."

The second principle calls for accountability from executive leaders "for supporting development of their own team members as well as developing the talent across the organization," says Shingleton. A key principle manifest throughout the leadership development efforts is that "the assessment of leadership talent is balanced and broad based" and that performance feedback is "supported with specific behavioral examples." In addition, the goal is to have a leadership team that reflects the diversity of Virginia Mason's staff and community.

The process is guided by the principle that executive leadership is accountable for ensuring "ready-now" candidates are immediately available whenever a leadership vacancy occurs. "We develop our leaders so that every year they are learning new things, taking on special assignments, rotating into a new area," says Shingleton. "If you are a leader here your resume gets better every year." The leadership identification process is comprehensive and ongoing. Clinicians and nonclinicians alike identified as potential leaders receive carefully drawn development plans to accelerate their growth. When executives gather to conduct talent reviews the discussion is confidential and led by Kaplan. The supervisor of the person being reviewed will offer a brief summary based on a structured prereview conversation they have had with the leader who reports to them. Discussed is formal training, current role, level of VMPS training, strengths, weaknesses, and aspirations. Says Charleen Tachibana, senior vice president and hospital administrator:

> Then everybody adds to that from their personal experience with the individual. We talk about what development opportunities might be, whether the person might have potential for greater

levels of leadership. The discussions are done in a very, very respectful manner. This approach creates a shared *knowledge* of who's out there and what their talent is. It's a way for the whole team to look across the organization and identify where we have talent depth, where we might have weaknesses, how we might redeploy people. Sometimes it might mean a temporary assignment to give the person a different exposure that they wouldn't normally get in their routine job.

A critical aspect of this work is identifying emerging physician leaders. Part of the leadership development process is driven by a small talent guiding team composed of a half-dozen top executives including both the CEO and COO. This team asks all physician leaders at Virginia Mason to identify doctors they believe can be future leaders. "Every current physician leader submits a short list of potential leaders within their area," says Shingleton. "The list of prospects is vetted by the guiding team. Once the list is whittled down all of the leadership candidates are discussed at a meeting of the three dozen top executives. For each physician we identify three strengths and three development opportunities."

In addition, a program called the Leadership Development Intensive, which is relatively new at Virginia Mason, brings together a select group of potential leaders for intensive teamwork over an eight-month period. "These are high potential folks we want to groom—five physician leaders and five nonphysician leaders," says Shingleton. Those selected are assigned a coach, undergo a 360-degree assessment, and begin rigorous classroom work. The Leadership Development Intensive is described internally as "an accelerated leadership development program for administrative and physician leaders that show potential to move up one to two levels over time. The Intensive focuses on the development of strategic agility, financial acumen, change leadership, and emotional intelligence to create a pipeline of leaders of the future." It is designed for

- New administrative directors
- Emerging physician leaders
- Directors
- Nonexecutive physician leaders
- Exceptionally high-performing managers

What defines a high potential leader?

The person is capable of taking on assignments with considerably greater scope and responsibility, typically with the potential to move up one or two levels in the organization over time. He/she displays a *high level* of:

- *Aspiration*: The degree to which the person truly *wants* to advance;
- *Ability*: The degree to which the person has the knowledge, skills, mental agility, and emotional intelligence to perform successfully;
- *Engagement*: The degree to which the person is committed to VMMC and willingly invests time and energy to go "above and beyond" the call of duty; and
- *Learning Agility*: The person possesses self-awareness, resilience, and resourcefulness, and delivers desired results in first-time situations through positive team-building

"Those who are selected for the program meet as a cohort for training classes," says Shingleton. "They work in two teams of five, and each team includes both physicians and administrators. Each team takes on a significant assignment—difficult challenges at a particular clinic or department for example." (All of this work is in addition to the team members' regular jobs.) Once the teams have completed their project work, they present the results in a forum open to the entire organization.

Ready-Now Leaders

At its core, talent review and leadership development are about succession planning. "We look at positions in the organization that are critical and we look at their projection," says Shingleton. "In talent review people tell us how much longer they plan to work. When someone is planning on retiring in 2016, for example, we make sure we have somebody in line to fill that role in 2016. Ideally, we have two or three who are being groomed for each role so that we have at least one or two *ready-now* candidates for every executive-level position, including physician leaders." It is important to note that the leadership development work at

Virginia Mason is not confined to the top executives. In fact, says Shingleton, "we go down three levels of leadership."

Shingleton laments what she views as a trend in recent years toward rapid turnover among executives in health care. She believes that a key element of Virginia Mason's leadership stability stems from the sustained opportunities leaders have to broaden their horizons and deepen their learning. "When you have rapid turnover—CEOs changing every three years or so—you can't have consistent development. We have a stable talent pipeline that secures our future, and that is really the purpose of talent development—to secure our future. Our planning helps ensure that the transformational work of the last decade and more is not just during my tenure in office or my leadership team's tenure but goes on in perpetuity."

Dr. Joyce Lammert, Hospital Medical Director

In September 2000, the Virginia Mason culture began its evolution to a very new place when doctors gathered for a retreat. Kaplan knew significant change was needed: that the traditional sense of entitlement among doctors had to give way to a new culture in which physicians would be great team members and leaders. But dictating what the change should be and how it would come about would have been a mistake and Kaplan knew it. He asked Lammert to pull the retreat together, and she did so skillfully. During the retreat there was much discussion about the changes coming in physicians lives. For many doctors there, recalls Lammert, there was a sense of loss, a feeling that something for which they had worked their whole professional lives—a sense of primacy and autonomy—was about to go away.

After the retreat, Kaplan asked Lammert to take on a particularly difficult leadership assignment: to lead a small committee charged with writing a Physician Compact. "I've known Joyce since she was an intern in internal medicine," recalls Kaplan. "She became a superb allergist and immunologist, highly respected clinically, and leader of the allergy clinic. I always thought she was a great thinker and a great people person. When the time came soon after my election as CEO to keep one of my campaign promises—which was to have a physician retreat for first time in many years—I turned to Joyce to lead the retreat. But she was a reluctant leader. She was not clamoring for leadership."

Both Kaplan and Lammert knew from the start the process of creating the document would be as important as the compact itself. This proved the essential power of the compact that eventually emerged. But it was far from easy. Lammert and her committee colleagues worked intensively for six months, meeting with physicians and listening carefully. Many of these conversations were painful. The sense of loss among doctors was raw. Lammert held scores of conversations—many quite intense marked by anger, resignation, and loss.

After six months of discussions, Lammert and her committee wrote a draft of a compact, then went through an arduous process of taking the draft compact to every department and discussing it with physicians. This was no simple matter, surely no rubber stamp. There were revisions to the draft, and there was some unhappiness. But at the end of the process Lammert and her committee had a document that the physicians at Virginia Mason were willing to sign onto, adhere to, live by, and be held accountable for. Recalls Lammert:

> It was a really tough assignment. We were a physician-centered kind of place because the whole practice was designed around physicians. The Physician Compact, which was happening sort of the same time as the Strategic Plan, was like hitting the reset button. And you have to change culture, but it has to happen in an evolutionary way. It was important to talk about it and do what we did with the retreat. We got to very explicit language about what the deal is *now* as opposed to what it used to be. That doesn't *change* culture but it makes you have that discussion.
>
> I was sort of a reluctant leader, and I certainly never thought about leadership when I started out. But I realized after leading the compact work (1) that leadership was something that people actually did and (2) that you could actually learn some of it. That it wasn't just nature—that you could actually learn how to be a leader. And I think that's when I really first said, "Wow, maybe I could do this."

With her work on the compact, says Kaplan, "Joyce showed herself to be a great leader." Soon he had a new assignment for her. General Internal Medicine (GIM) was Virginia Mason's largest clinic site. Says Kaplan:

> It was a mess. There was no flow, there were long waits, morale was in the gutter, and there was no obvious new leader. So I looked for my most underleveraged strong leader even if from outside GIM. This was the first time I appointed a section head from out-side the section. Almost all the general internists objected, but within three months there was unanimity and consensus in the section that she was the best leader they ever had. She learned what motivated everybody—nurses, doctors, medical assistants, flow managers.

After several years at GIM, it was clear Lammert could handle any leadership assignment, and Kaplan appointed her chief of medi-cine where, says Kaplan, "she did a fabulous job."

Leanne Lewis, Administrative Director, Anatomic Pathology and Clinical Laboratories

Lewis began her Virginia Mason career fresh out of college in 1985 working in the credit department of patient financial ser-vices. After five years in various positions including supervisor of the billing team, she left Virginia Mason for another oppor-tunity. But by 1999 she was back—this time as a manager in the same department in which she had first started. In 2001, when the organization began to adapt the Toyota Production System, Lewis dipped her toe into various improvement events, includ-ing her first Rapid Process Improvement Workshop. She was for-tunate to have a manager in Steve Schaefer, vice president, who encouraged all staff members to engage and participate in lean education. As Schaefer was getting more involved in the Virginia Mason Production System he would bring his team along with him. "There was a lot of reading he was doing for his certification and he would have us do the reading as well," she says. "That's why our department was an early adopter of VMPS."

Several years into the lean journey, Lewis earned her certification as a VMPS leader and sought to create a system of standard work within patient financial services. Traditionally, employees within the department who worked collecting payments owed to Virginia Mason would have a series of collection assignments for the day. At any given time one staff member might be working to collect an account worth $10,000 while another teammate might be seeking to collect $300. Lewis and her colleagues applied VMPS principles and tools and changed things around. Production boards make work visible to all team members, something that had never before been the case within the department. And new production boards showed the account balances each team member was working on at any given moment.

One result of the old system was that when a staff member was done completing his or her collections for the day, the person would then be assigned additional work. Staff members would take note that another staffer didn't complete work nearly as quickly, and there was some simmering resentment. What none of the staffers knew was exactly how much anyone was going after at any given time. Once they knew that—through highly visible production boards—it helped everyone understand the nature of the work. It also helped create a stronger sense of shared mission and teamwork. When the production board showed, for example, that one staff member was working to collect $30,000 and someone else $3,000, staff members would be shifted over to assist the worker with the largest amount outstanding. After a very short period of time staff members did not have to be told to do this— they acted on their own. The result was a more efficient use of resources by an aligned, connected team rather than work by a group of individuals.

Lewis had worked in the financial end of health care for nearly 25 years when she was asked to consider a significant change. Sue Anderson, Virginia Mason executive vice president and chief financial officer, sat down with Lewis and suggested that she take a position within the Kaizen Promotion Office. Lewis had completed a Virginia Mason fellowship during which she had engaged in deep learning about VMPS (which included a trip to Japan). "Sue was a firm believer that as a leader you need to expand your scope, to learn more about other value streams across the organization and how they connect," says Lewis. Through the talent review process, Kaplan was well aware of Lewis's work. "Leanne was a great analyst in finance, and she was identified by her supervisor [Schaefer], who saw she had great potential," says Kaplan. "She went to KPO and was fabulous there."

She was attracted to the idea of going to KPO to work on improvement projects in areas other than patient financial services. "I think if you are going to go outside your realm you should push," she says. "I didn't want to oversee a process I already knew at a very detailed level." Lewis's tenure in KPO would run to slightly more than two years, and the goal from the start was "to expand your knowledge as a leader and understand the organization and its connectivity across all of the value streams." Says Kathy Shingleton: "In Patient Financial Services Leanne supervised 200 people. Then she goes over to KPO and has no staff. So you are learning to lead through influence and collaboration. It's not about hierarchies. KPO is where you learn a whole different set of leadership skills can be applied to variety of other areas."

For Lewis and others who went to KPO, this was an essential lesson: that gaining expertise in the method and tools of improvement allows you to work in any area of the organization. Traditionally, a person assigned to improve work in the operating room, for example, would be someone with deep knowledge of and experience in the OR. But that was not the case at Virginia Mason and not the case with the application of the Toyota method. "Working in KPO promotes the feeling that you can learn something new and do something different," says Lewis, and she did just that by working on improvement in the clinic, an area with which she had minimal familiarity. "If you have the improvement skill set you can look at a process and work with the team to improve it," she says.

A major part of her work focused on standard work for leaders within primary care and specialty clinics. In primary care in particular there was a challenge understanding what caused physicians to get out of flow—and behind schedule—and how to get them back into flow. She worked to help create standard work for leaders enabling physicians with team support to stay in flow or, when out of it, to get back on track. A breakthrough moment for Lewis came when she traveled to the United Kingdom to coach an improvement workshop. She met with the hospital leader there and discovered that he was using RPIWs to spread standard work throughout several different hospitals. "It's a great concept," says Lewis. "How can we take standard work we have developed and do a better job spreading it across primary care?"

Back in Seattle, she led kaizen events at the various clinical sites, adjusting the standard work based on the varying staffing models in the clinics. Historically, standard work rollout has been uneven and inconsistent across primary care teams. Knowledge of an RPIW at one site did not ensure meaningful training and rollout at other locations. The concept of *share and spread* was an attempt to ensure knowledge and training were consistently applied. In 2011, the share and spread kaizen events were used to spread the work of keeping the provider in flow. Each primary care team had the same metrics to improve, though site specific, to reflect their own improvement activity based on the new standard processes. The notion of taking process skills into an area one has never before experienced at any depth was put to the test with Lewis, when after her KPO stint, she was appointed administrative director of the laboratory where she oversaw all lab functions including anatomic pathology, hematology, microbiology, chemistry and more. The department operates 24 hours a day, seven days a week and includes about 230 employees.

The fact that Lewis slipped into the position and was comfortable as the lab leader in a very short period of time is testament to the precept that knowledge of process improvement and leadership can trump subject matter knowledge. If the question was whether you would rather have a great lab person as lab leader or a great leader and improvement expert then the choice was easy. She led a series of improvements including in some cases a reduction in turnaround times of as much as 30 percent. "Leanne did a great job in KPO and became head of the lab," says Kaplan. "Previously that job had been held only by people with lab experience and a clinical background. It speaks to the theme that leaders, before the fact, don't have to be content experts or of the same professional tribe. They can learn. It's more about leadership than being a member of the tribe."

Katerie Chapman, Vice President Surgical and Procedural Care and Support Services

Things were going very well for Chapman. Barely a few years out of graduate school she had already achieved certification in VMPS, was leading RPIWs, and serving as administrative director of the Heart Institute. She had made the all-important pilgrimage to Japan to learn the Toyota method in a factory and experience Toyota Production System (TPS) in its purest form. And she had found that adapting the TPS to health care felt intuitive to her. "I was young, very new, and relatively immature in my leadership, so I just adopted VMPS as my management method," she recalls. "I never had to relearn a style or method because I had come in at a time where I could just absorb the new approach."

Things could not have been going better—and then she got tapped on the shoulder in the form of an email from Kaplan. There had been speculation about who among the up-and-comers would be asked to detour into the Kaizen Promotion Office for two to three years of work—a prospect Chapman dreaded:

> It was my birthday, and I was supposed to be having a good day. I was in my office, one I shared with a couple of people at that time, and I got an email from Gary. I knew immediately that it involved my going to KPO. I did *not* want to go. I had no interest in going. I started as an intern, and I was now an administrative director. And I'd been in the organization only a couple years. I was on a path. I wanted to be an executive, and I believed I just needed to stay on that path. I got this message, and I knew immediately what it meant. And my first response was not positive. I did not receive it positively. I thought, "This is going to derail my career. I am not doing this. I'm going to get stuck over there doing project work."

She spoke with several executives, and "eventually I realized that it would be a pretty career-limiting move to decline. It'd be like saying 'I don't *believe* in VMPS enough to go to KPO. I don't trust the leaders of the organization enough to go over there." Recalls Kaplan:

> Katerie was very smart and talented and very interested in career development. She was the line leader in cardiology, and we went to her and said, "You need to be one of the first administrative directors to go to KPO." She was aghast. The standard pathway in health care administration is to continue to progress and develop in operations and ultimately assume executive responsibilities. I said, "Katerie, trust us. This will be fabulous training and fabulous learning, and this would be the new pathway."

In conversations with senior leaders the message to Chapman was that this was a very good career move because all future leaders will have deep knowledge and expertise in VMPS. Says Chapman, "I knew I had opportunities for greater levels of learning and understanding, there wasn't any question about that. I was just hoping to do it as a leader within a clinical setting."

After her initial reaction abated, and after thoughtful conversations, she realized that the assignment was a significant vote of confidence in her potential leadership ability within the organization. "I realized that they were taking a leap of faith with me," she says. "So I kind of felt compelled to say, 'You have given me great opportunities, and if this is what you want me to do, I'll do it.' Even though I kind of dreaded it a little I said, 'Yes, I will go and do this.' The reality was I had trust in the leadership. They had given me opportunities and fostered my growth. They had invested in me, and I deeply appreciate that." Some years later, she says there is no question that "it was the best move of my career."

Developing leadership talent in a careful, unorthodox fashion is essential to Virginia Mason's success. Plucking promising leaders from roles where they have demonstrated talent and moving them to KPO provides them with a challenge and an opportunity with responsibility—along with operational leaders—for strategy and implementation of VMPS. "In KPO I had exposure to parts of the organization that I never would have had otherwise," says

Chapman. "You gain an in-depth understanding not only of the principles and tools of VMPS but also of how it can transform teams, processes, and outcomes. I wouldn't have had that level of exposure or that time to really invest in my own development in that same way had I been in the Heart Institute, trying to lead operations and learn."

As she began work at KPO Chapman was initially quite frustrated. "I didn't have my hand on the lever. When I was leading in my operational area I could drive the changes; I had the authority. In KPO, you don't have that same authority. It became a great leadership lesson and developing competency for me—learning how to lead through influence." Essential to leadership training for Chapman and others who worked within KPO was the richness of their experiences working in a wide variety of departments across the medical center. Part of that richness was that Chapman and others at KPO were developing the structure for how the organization would lead with VMPS. Virginia Mason has made significant progress at knocking down siloes, although this is a never-ending battle in almost any provider organization. But the organization was clearly more siloed back around 2005 when Chapman joined KPO.

"Two types of exposure were critical to my development at that time," she recalls. "One was exposure to different parts of the organization and the other was exposure to executives. That was huge. Not only did I get an opportunity to interact with more of them, but also I was visible to them. They could see my strengths, areas of opportunity, how I think and work. That exposure is critical." The irony for Chapman is that had she remained on her preferred path, she would not have had the enriching experience of engaging in a wide variety of improvement projects across the organization—an experience that significantly enhanced her knowledge base, relationships, and ability to lead. She says without the KPO experience it would have taken her many years to gain the amount of cross-organization experience she achieved in just two years in KPO.

When she was nearing the end of her time at KPO the question arose: Where would she go next? She had proven herself an adept leader, and it was important to find the right place where she would be effective while at the same time have a chance to grow as a manager and leader. An explicit goal of KPO is to develop

VMPS leaders and then return them to operations to accelerate the pace of transformation. Coincidentally, the administrative director of perioperative services decided to leave the position just when Chapman was having discussions with senior executives about where she would land next. Tachibana told Chapman she thought the perioperative services position was right for her. But Chapman was unsure. She had proven to be a strong improvement leader, but she was not a clinician and the perioperative position had traditionally been held by a nurse. "Charleen said to me, 'No, you're not a nurse. But I don't *need* a nurse. I need someone that can *lead* with VMPS in such a critical location in this organization.'"

Dr. Donna Smith, Medical Director of Clinic

Although Smith never thought of herself as a leader, she had held a series of modest leadership roles in her pediatric group, and when the group joined Virginia Mason in 1996 she became the deputy chief of pediatrics. Soon thereafter, Kaplan asked her to take over as chief of pediatrics. "I remember thinking at the time that I had not identified myself as passionate about leadership or that it was something I was particularly good at," Smith says. In medical school, she had been a leader on various work or study teams, but she didn't contemplate then that she would take a leadership role as a practicing physician.

As was the case with Lammert, Kaplan saw something in Smith. "Donna was a great pediatrician, the clinical leader of the most highly regarded pediatric group in Seattle," recalls Kaplan. In the mid-1990s Smith's group joined Virginia Mason and Kaplan says he "soon saw tremendous leadership skills from her and within a couple of years she was chief of pediatrics for the whole institution. Donna is very strong clinically, very trustworthy, and a very good thinker." This was in 2001, a pivotal time in Virginia Mason's history, for it was just as the organization was developing both the Strategic Plan and the Physician Compact. Smith was in the cauldron with the rest of the team when Kaplan led Virginia Mason on the inaugural Japan journey. "Along with the rest of the executive team I got to wrestle with the question of, 'Are we going to do this? Is it going to be effective? Are we all in? What are we afraid of?'"

The first Japan trip, as it turned out, served as intensive leadership training. Working on the factory floor in an alien culture with a significant language barrier was stressful. On top of that, the team knew that they would have to make a collective decision on whether this was the right path for Virginia Mason—a path that was, to understate it, a radical departure for how to govern an American health care organization.

For all the stress and pressure, however, Smith felt a sense of stability and a certain clarity in large measure thanks to rigorous study, discussion and training before the Japan trip. A few years later Kaplan called upon her once more to expand her leadership portfolio. "He called me into his office and said, 'What would you think about taking on a leadership role in an area not in pediatrics? Outside your expertise?' And I said it would depend on the area and what the issues are." They had a couple of discussions, and Kaplan told her he wanted her to remain as chief of pediatrics while also taking leadership responsibility for the emergency department. "In pediatrics she was underleveraged," says Kaplan. "There was a dysfunctional work unit similar to General Internal Medicine where Joyce became the leader. So I appointed Donna, chief of pediatrics, in an emergency room that doesn't take care of children. The ER docs thought I had lost my mind, but within six months Donna was creating major, large-scale change."

When she started the emergency department leadership position, Smith says:

> I felt totally out of my comfort zone. I wanted to be really clear—
> "How do I engage and support this team? How do I use the tools
> of VMPS to make things visual?" It was definitely a stretch, but
> there was work to do and when there's work to do it helps provide
> laser focus. Working across historical boundaries using VMPS
> we improved systems to eliminate hospital diverts, reduce door
> to physician time and length of stay. The team partnered with the
> medics in the community and the cath lab internally to dramati-
> cally reduce door to balloon time and significantly improve qual-
> ity of care for people having a heart attack.

Smith made a discovery. While she did not know the work of the Emergency Department in any great depth—having never worked in emergency medicine—she realized that she *did* know how to lead. "It was not work I was familiar with and knew how to do, but I found I could lead and engage all the team members," she says. "I learned more about systems thinking across the organization and the power of creating cross continuum teams." The key is to create systems and processes that "set people up for success," she says. "We were partnering with people and taking minutes and hours off procedures and increasing quality exponentially. We really started to work multidisciplinary teams together—nursing, patient care technicians, medics, and physicians at the bedside."

After working in the ED and as chief of pediatrics, Kaplan appointed Smith as hospital medical director where she partnered in a dyad with the chief nursing officer.

In early 2013, Kaplan asked Smith to take on a new role—medical director of the clinics—including the departments of surgery, medicine, primary care, radiology, and pathology. This would be a significant expansion of responsibility and Smith needed a weekend to think about it—with good reason. At that time she was also serving as the physician executive in charge of patient experience and hospital medical director. *And* she was enrolled in graduate school to earn a master of business administration. Convinced it could help her become a better leader, 22 years after her graduation from medical school she was pursuing an MBA. She did it, in fact, for the patients. She was in her final six months of the program with a load of work ahead—papers and exams—yet over the weekend she decided she would accept the new position.

The MBA program at Seattle University, a Jesuit institution, "was framed by social justice and contemplation in action," she says. " It was very much about community benefit. From a values perspective it was very consistent with how I think." She completed the MBA program as she grew comfortable in her role leading the clinics working alongside a strong administrative partner in Jim Cote. As Smith considers the nature of her leadership progression, she offers an important insight: "The power of having somebody who sees potential in you is a lesson for all of us—what it does to build your confidence. We have to remember that every day seeing the potential in others and helping them grow fuels them. When others have confidence in you it builds your confidence in yourself, and Gary knows I appreciate him beyond measure for that."

Shelly Fagerlund, Vice President, Clinic Operations

"When I was working in Salt Lake City I felt like we weren't doing a great job as a society around delivering health care to people who need it because we cost too much," says Fagerlund. "I have a little streak of social justice—that we do better as a society when we make health care more accessible. We did some very good work in Salt Lake City. There is no shortage of ideas or attempts to make things better, but for me seeing the difference with the Virginia Mason Production System showed we can chart our own course and says that the status quo isn't acceptable and we're going to change it. And we are not going to wait for anybody else to tell us how to proceed." Fagerlund had spent much of her career in health care in Salt Lake City working with excellent people at various organizations including an academic medical center and community health system. She joined Virginia Mason in 1997 as a manager in human resources. She advanced quickly to a director's role and embraced the opportunity to lead.

When a sense of quiet excitement began to build among leaders during 2001 as teams explored the Toyota Production System, Fagerlund saw it as a possible "paradigm shift in how we would lead." But she was also cautious. "I had been in enough health care organizations to know we could get excited about something and then quickly move on to something else." Fagerlund was among the first dozen or so Virginia Mason leaders to go through the new certification process—enabling her to lead a variety of kaizen events—early on. She found the Toyota methods and tools empowering. "VMPS enabled us to work on improvement with urgency and speed—to get in and get out. And I really loved that."

Fagerlund had spent her entire professional life in health care human resources, but that changed in 2005 when she was asked to manage an ambulatory care practice. She immediately embraced the opportunity. "Even though I didn't know a lot about how to run a clinic, I did know how to engage with people and some of the lean concepts—to be on the genba, be visible and present, and study your processes." She worked on the basics—checking patients in for their appointments and physician schedules, for example—looking for ways to improve efficiency and eliminate wastes, especially of time. "I had to get super granular with the frontline processes, asking a lot of questions," she says. "It was tremendously helpful to me to get grounded in a new set of responsibilities."

As she started her VMPS work, Fagerlund wanted to determine where, exactly, there was additional or underused capacity within the clinics. She ran workshops to examine value streams and thus identify staff members with additional capacity and moved them into a new assignment that would allow them to be more productive. "We worked to make sure you landed in a position where you could use your skills and abilities," she says. Fagerlund was identified through the talent review process as a leader with significant potential. And the question arose, as it had with Chapman and Lewis: Should she do a rotation in KPO? "I thought there is no way I can do that," she recalls. And her barrier was quite similar to Smith's: Fagerlund, after 21 years in the health care business, was in the process of seeking a graduate degree. "I was working on my master's in organizational development, and I didn't know if I could take on a KPO rotation," she recalls. "The question on my mind was, 'If I do it, what am I in for?'"

She discussed just that with Chapman and others and after those conversations and some reflection, she decided she could handle it, even though she was barely through the first quarter of her degree program. "The organizational commitment was, 'Where can we best use you, and where do you have the most passion?'" The shift was a bit jarring initially. A significant aspect of the KPO role is to stand up in front of the entire executive leadership team every Tuesday morning and report on the progress or lack thereof of various improvement initiatives. This is by no means a pro forma session. It is fast-paced, and the questions from senior executives—including from the CEO—can be pointed.

"You need to be on your game, be crisp and articulate and tell the story," she says. "You have 7 minutes for your report at each standup." She learned quickly at KPO that her leadership coin of the realm was influence. She had held many management roles where she had clear authority over other staff members, but at KPO "you realize nothing gets done unless you use influence to form a partnership. If you do not have effective working relationships with people throughout the organization then you are not moving the needle." She reflects upon this for a moment and then adds:

> That was not always a smooth process. You have to figure out when to push and when to step back and when to support and empathize and exhort. I walked in to KPO with a perception that I would have to become a deep kaizen sensei, but it was not that. It is all about how to create the right portfolio of improvement work to achieve the results the business needs. What is the right pace of change? You are looking for shelf space with a particular operations leaders who needs to be at the table to drive the improvement work with you.

Kaplan says that when Fagerlund initially came to Virginia Mason she was "kind of quiet and shy. But she has continuously looked for new ways to learn and develop. She has very good people skills, is a clear thinker and someone people enjoy working with." One of her ideas was to subject the KPO process itself to a value-stream examination. This was triggered by the unrelenting pressure of gathering, packaging, and presenting reports from a variety of improvement initiatives at Tuesday morning standup. Week after week she was the one at the wall having had to invest a great deal of preparation for 7 minutes of presenting. The idea was to conduct a kaizen event to improve the KPO Tuesday report-out preparation process as well as the visibility of the overall improvement portfolio process. One result was a more even distribution of the prep work within KPO, which reduced waste of time and improved quality.

"The KPO role for me was transformative," she says. "I would do it again in a heartbeat."

Chapter 7

A *Very* Different Kind of Board

Case 1: Optical Implant Error

Members of the Virginia Mason board of directors received the news of the error 24 hours after the mistake occurred. The patient was scheduled for two consecutive procedures in the same eye. After the first surgeon operated and left the operating room to dictate notes, he realized he had implanted the wrong size lens in the patient's eye. He went back to the OR, reported what had happened, and corrected the mistake.

This case resulted in a red patient safety alert (PSA), and all such alerts are promptly reported to board members. In this case, the analysis of what had gone wrong was simple. Two implants—different sizes—were side by side on a tray in the OR. The corrective action was obvious: create standard work to ensure that only the lens being used in that surgery is permitted in the OR. Thus, a simple matter of physically separating the implants and communicating about the size to be inserted became part of communication during the presurgical timeout.

The question is: Why is the Virginia Mason board of directors involved in the details of this matter?

Case 2: Billing Chaos

Board members received word of a mistake concerning a child needing separate surgeries for a hearing issue. Before the first operation, the child's mother asked the Virginia Mason team whether the surgery would be covered by insurance. A staff member checked with the insurance company and was assured the answer was yes.

But not long after the surgery the mother received a bill for $35,000 from Virginia Mason. It turned out that the insurance company said that the surgery was not covered under the family's policy. Then came a tug-of-war between Virginia Mason and the insurance plan, with each side contradicting the other. The insurance company said it made it clear to Virginia Mason that the procedure was not covered. A Virginia Mason staff member said the insurer explicitly approved the procedure. Fortunately, there was a recording of the conversation confirming that the insurance company had, in fact, approved the surgery. But the story gets worse.

"The second surgery actually had to be postponed because of the disagreement over coverage," says board chair Jim Young. "And without the second surgery the child would have been unable to hear out of one ear." Again the question: Why was the Virginia Mason board deeply involved in a billing issue with an insurance company? And the answer is because it was not really about a billing issue. It was about the patient and family experience of care, and on this one Virginia Mason had fallen far short of its own standards. Yes, in a way, it was the insurance company's "fault." But the fact was that the confusion placed tremendous stress on the family—stress that was entirely unnecessary and avoidable if Virginia Mason had had a much sturdier and more reliable process in place.

If we step back and ask what leadership looks like, we see a board chair and his members deeply engaged in what might appear at other organizations to be yet another billing disagreement. Yet to Young and his colleagues, the surface issue was billing procedure—which ended up being easily solved with standard work. The much larger issue for Young and his colleagues was the patient and his family. To the board this was about the quality of a child's life. "Without the second surgery the child would not be able to hear out of one ear, and think about the problems that would cause in a classroom, for example," says Young. "Think about the ambient noise in any situation like that. The child kept saying to his parents, 'When am I going to have the second operation so I can hear?'"

The child's mother was invited to a board meeting where she conveyed the enormous frustration and stress the family experienced throughout the ordeal. Hearing these sorts of stories from patients—as the board does at the start of every meeting—keeps the members hyperfocused on patients. "When anything goes wrong at Virginia Mason, I know immediately what happened and what is being done," says board member Julie Morath. "Those events are not closed until the board says they are. This is not a rubber stamp board."

"We needed to have standard work around insuring that when somebody has surgery that without doubt the patient knows whether the insurance company is going to pay for it," says Young. "Before it was all verbal. Now we have a standard form that takes all the risk out of it. This was egregious miscommunication."

Case 3: Failure to Recognize Emergent Symptoms

In the first two case studies, the corrective action proposed by staff was straightforward and readily approved by the board. While that is the norm with red PSAs, there are exceptions. There are cases where staff-level root-cause analysis of a red PSA generates a fix that is rejected by the board as insufficient. "Go back and find a better way" is the message.

Fielding calls from patients is not a simple matter. Staff members on the phones, who have no clinical background, deal with many issues. Patients call in reporting a wide variety of maladies from very minor to quite serious. It is clear to the phone staff how to handle the great majority of calls: Set up a clinic appointment, refer to a nurse specialist, send the patient to the Emergency Department, or call 911. But there is also a gray area where discerning how sick a patient might be—over the telephone—is tricky.

Staff members in the call center make very few mistakes, but any mistake where a serious symptom is missed is deeply concerning.

When it became clear in 2011 that too many callers with potentially serious symptoms were not detected, a red PSA was declared. In a number of instances, call center staff failed to discern symptoms that should have been recognized as potentially serious. In these cases patients were scheduled for later clinic appointments when they should have been immediately transferred to a nurse for a deeper assessment. This would ensure that the medical issue would be addressed appropriately and that if the patient experienced symptoms indicating a potentially serious event then the patient was seen right away. The call center issue, though it did not cause harm to any patient, was recognized as a risky situation with the potential to harm patients—thus the red PSA.

What does a call center problem, an OR error, or a billing dispute have to do with the board of directors? And the answer is *everything*. The mission to keep patients safe is sacrosanct at Virginia Mason—the medical center's foundational duty. The PSA system has worked remarkably well through the years to improve safety. Metrics and many awards attest to the level of safety at Virginia Mason. And there is this somewhat amazing fact: the leader of the National Health Service in Great Britain journeyed from London to Seattle to announce that he was instituting a Virginia Mason like safety program in his country.

There are countless reasons that Virginia Mason has become safer. One of those is the direct, hands-on involvement of the board in every red PSA. Only the board has the authority to close red PSAs—that is, to determine that the problem presented has been solved, that the root cause has been determined, and that standard work is in place to make sure that particular problem is mistake-proof. Thus, board members receive bad news promptly, and they remain directly engaged with whatever the issue happens to be from that moment until the issue is fully resolved—weeks, months, even years later.

The urgent–emergent program for the call center is much stronger now because of the relentless pursuit of excellence from the board. Doctors worked to create algorithms in which key words would trigger action by the call center, or any other employee who answered a call from a patient.

A *Very* Different Kind of Board

It would be difficult to overstate the importance of the board to Virginia Mason. It was the directors, after all, who challenged Dr. Gary Kaplan and his team on the issue of whether Virginia Mason was a patient-centered organization. And it was because of the board's insistence that management concluded that, in fact, far too often patients' interests were subordinated to the interests of physicians and staff. That was perhaps the pivotal moment in the modern Virginia Mason journey. And it was the board that had the vision and courage to alter the governance rules to make the CEO position appointed rather than elected. This move enabled Kaplan to lead the profound transformation at the organization. This is anything but a typical health care board.

Significant demands are put on board members. Each year there is a board retreat as well as six other meetings. In addition, each board member must go through an education process to learn the essential elements of the Virginia Mason Production System. And all board members are required to go on a two-week trip to Japan with Kaplan to work in a manufacturing plant at the most basic level. The trip is a fundamental part of each member's ability to understand lean management and lean tools. But it is no vacation. The Japan trip is an essential element of the board experience. Kaplan leads a Virginia Mason team of board members, physician, and administrative leaders to Japan every June and has done so for 12 consecutive years. The trip is so sacrosanct that any board member failing to make the journey during his or her first term is ineligible for reappointment to the board. The trip is absolutely necessary for it exposes board members (and others) to the front lines of the Toyota Production System. Board members work with others in teams on the factory floor focused on challenging assignments. It serves as a valuable shared experience for all board members. "Everyone on the trip is required to have a process they are working to improve in their area—how to apply lean to improve governance," says board member Jamie Orlikoff. "It is very, very challenging, and you are working to find a way to improve the governance process as you are in this manufacturing facility seeing lean management in action. They work you very hard, and it is challenging."

Board members possess two types of skills: expertise and literacy. Carolyn Corvi, for example, the former Boeing executive and current Virginia Mason board member, had deep expertise in lean management, having used that approach in the construction of the Boeing 737 line of commercial aircraft. Most board members, Orlikoff notes, possess the other type of competency—literacy:

> You cannot educate a board member to a level of expertise, says Orlikoff. They either have it or they don't. But you can educate someone to a standard of literacy, and on our board it is clear that every member must be literate in lean management. We want every board member to be at high level of literacy in lean, and I would say our high level translates into an expert level in many other organizations. That is the reason for the required Japan trip so that every board member has a deep level of literacy.
>
> The board personality is one of inquiry. We have constructive dissent and we disagree—sometimes sharply—without being disagreeable. There is a real appreciation on our board for constructive dissent. We really discourage hallway conversations. If anyone has an issue to bring up they do so in an atmosphere of open communication.

The influence of the Virginia Mason board suggests the leverage that boards of other health care organizations have to transform their own organizations. Visitors frequently ask Virginia Mason leaders, How can I get my C-suite leaders to adapt the Virginia Mason Production System? There are a number of ways to do it, but certainly one powerful lever could be board members who urge executives in that direction. This rarely happens, but one wonders why? Why are boards among the most underutilized levers to transform health care? Why are they so often so passive?

The Virginia Mason Board is composed largely of professionals from the Greater Seattle area including the following:

James Young, board chair, was the managing partner of the Seattle office of Grant Thornton LLP, the fifth largest international accounting tax and business advisory firm. He retired in 2006.

Jane Blodgett retired from Ernst & Young in 2010, where she most recently served as the office managing partner for the Seattle and Portland offices.

Michelle Burris is an experienced pharmaceutical company executive who formerly held strategic and operations planning positions at Boeing.

Carolyn Corvi has served as Virginia Mason Board member and chair for 13 years. She is former vice president-general manager of Airplane Programs, Boeing Commercial Airplanes where she led Commercial Airplanes integrated production system-including design, production and delivery of the 737, 747, 767 and 777. She serves on the board of United Airlines among others and is co-founder of the Northwest Children's Fund.

Lewis S. (Lonnie) Edelheit, PhD, retired from General Electric Company in December 2001 after a successful tenure as GE's senior vice president of research and development and member of GE's Corporate Executive Council.

Joshua Green, III, is chairman and chief executive officer of the Joshua Green Corporation, a diversified investment company holding neighborhood shopping centers, office buildings, venture capital investments, and a diversified stock portfolio.

Tod R. Hamachek is former chair and CEO of Penwest Pharmaceuticals Co., from which he retired in 2005.

Dr. Gary Kaplan, Virginia Mason CEO.

Robert Lemon, treasurer, spent his entire 31-year business career with Accenture LLP (formerly Andersen Consulting), including 21 years as a partner, and he retired in 2003.

Al Lopus is the president and cofounder of the Best Workplaces, which provides research-based measurement tools and strategic advisory services to nonprofit organizations.

Richard Martinez is a Senior Vice President and Commercial Banking Manager for Northwest Bank.

Dorothy Mann, PhD, MPH, Secretary, is former regional health administrator of the U.S. Public Health Service. She served as chair of Group Health Cooperative and served on the board of Kaiser Permanente Health Plan.

Mary McWilliams has held many leadership positions during her career in health care. She formerly served as Executive Director of Washington Health Alliance (formerly Puget Sound Health Alliance) and as President and CEO of Regence BlueShield. She is a director and past chair of the Seattle Branch of the Federal Reserve Bank of San Francisco.

Kristi Pangrazio is owner of Artful Gifting and former chair of the board of the Hope Heart Institute.

Julie Morath, RN, MS, lives in San Francisco where she is senior vice president of California Hospital Association and CEO of the California Hospital Quality Institute. She formerly served as chief quality and safety officer for the Vanderbilt University Medical Center, chief operating officer of Children's Hospital's and Clinics of Minnesota, and system vice president of Allina Health System in Minnesota.

James Orlikoff, vice chair of the board, resides in Chicago. He is president of Orlikoff & Associates, Inc., a consulting firm specializing in health care governance and leadership, strategy, quality, organizational development, and risk management. He is senior consultant to the Center for Healthcare Governance and is the National Advisor on Governance and Leadership to the American Hospital Association and Health Forum. He was named one of the 100 most powerful people in health care in the inaugural list by *Modern Healthcare* magazine.

Jamie Brings a Unique Level of Health Care Expertise

Orlikoff is an unusual board member on two counts. He is one of only two board members who does not live in the greater Seattle area. More significantly, he is widely recognized as one of the nation's leading experts on health care governance. He has worked with hundreds of health care organizations throughout the country advising and guiding boards on best practices. His work has ranged from Sentara in Virginia to Sutter in California—from Memorial Hermann, Houston, to Gundersen in LaCrosse, Wisconsin. He has worked with numerous associations including the National Quality Forum, American Hospital Association, American Board of Internal Medicine, the American Board of Radiology and more. And internationally he has consulted with organizations in Great Britain (including the National Health Service), Saudi Arabia, New Zealand, and Singapore, among others. His influence has been strong enough through the years that he was named one of the 100 most powerful people in health care in the inaugural list by *Modern Healthcare* magazine. "Jamie brings a unique level of health care expertise," says Young. "He sees things not just through a Virginia Mason lens but from a national perspective and from having had so many years of experience dealing with hundreds of different boards and their challenges."

Orlikoff says the Virginia Mason board aspires to be "a best practices board. Many, many health care boards ask the question: What do most boards do? They compare themselves to the norm, and when you do that you're attempting to become the cream of the crap. We try to ask what do the *best* boards do?"

Orlikoff notes that the first hospital board was founded in Philadelphia by Ben Franklin in 1752. "The idea was governance on behalf of the community," says Orlikoff, "which necessitates governance *by* members of that community. That concept worked wonderfully until the 1980s when it came to be a drawback." That drawback comes in the form of overly comfortable relationships between board members and leaders within the organization they are supposed to govern for the benefit of all patients. Too often board members seek to gain personal benefit from close association with leaders particularly leading physicians. The unfortunate reality in many areas is that prominent and wealthy individuals seek or accept board positions to gain an inside track to leading specialists, to rapid access, to an elite status that allows these board members and their families to receive special treatment. The implicit bargain is that the board members will do what they can to make the lives of hospital leaders comfortable so that access and special treatment are returned.

Interconnected personal relationships between board members and hospital executives and their physicians can be a barrier to the best interests of patients. When difficult choices have to be made—concerning a merger, layoffs, or action against a prominent doctor—sometimes community boards blink. Orlikoff has seen this firsthand. "There have been many cases where board members worried about making the difficult choices for fear of how they might be perceived in their community," he says. "I have seen many, many boards around the country knowing what they need to do but refusing because they are unwilling to take the social and political grief."

The Ben Franklin community model is no longer sufficient because of the complexity of health care as an industry. "A hospital is the most complex business model in human history according to Peter Drucker," says Orlikoff. " The business has become so complex that the odds are that you don't have all the skill sets within the local community you need to govern the hospital. Yet in many places they still require that board members must live within 25 miles of the headquarters. The pushback is very real on social issues in many communities." The solution is twofold: engage courageous community board members who place the patient above all other considerations and include board members who do not live in the community.

Rigorous Evaluations of Board Members

In light of his experience as a consultant for 25 years, Orlikoff is in a unique position to compare Virginia Mason's board to others. "We evaluate far more than other boards," he says. "We are always doing board evaluations, and individual member evaluations. This is how the board holds itself accountable."

Another unusual practice of the Virginia Mason board is that meetings happen in three different phases and have done so since about 2006.

- Level one comes for the first portion of the meeting when those present include all board members as well as executives, staff, and a patient–family telling their story.
- Level two includes board members and the CEO only.
- Finally, level three is confined to board members.

"When you go above a certain size you cannot have meaningful conversations," says Orlikoff. During level one a good deal gets accomplished including reports from staff as well as input from patients and families. At level two, "the board and the CEO can really start digging in and have honest confidential conversations. In level three—executive session—the board holds itself accountable. There are discussions about information and issues raised during the first two levels of the meeting: Have you thought of this? Why hasn't this been taken into account? While the conversations can be pointed, people generally do not get defensive because they feel a sense of comfort within a culture where getting at the reality is an honored process; and where the desire for truth is far weightier than any instinct to assess blame.

"Everybody sits around table with the same purpose: How do we get better? How do we improve?" says Orlikoff. "It is deep within the culture. The executive sessions allow the board to have honest and confidential conversations—'I didn't get this. Am I the only one?' We can share uncertainty, ask for further clarification. This enhances ownership of decisions we subsequently make." The three-level approach is uncommon in health care. While many boards go into executive session annually to review CEO performance, it is unusual to see it more regularly in large measure, says Orlikoff, "because many CEOs feel threatened by executive sessions."

A key aspect of the board's responsibility involves succession planning both at the executive and board level. "We are into competency-based selection—what are the skill sets essential to effective governance and we are trying to create the board of five years from now and that involves some serious thinking and discussion about where health care is going and what new skill sets we might need." Says board member Julie Morath, "It is a very thinking board, and we have the right mix of experience, knowledge, and skills to help advance the organization. The board is very involved and we have a healthy collaborative collegial spirit."

What does leadership look like? Board chair Jim Young says, "It is the ability of our organization including senior management and the board staying on the path of the Virginia Mason Production System and recognizing the fact that it is a journey and a journey without a destination because improvement is continuous." Young is emphatic when he states that the board's dedication to the Strategic Plan is "absolute and relentless. It is about totally being focused on the patient. Everything starts with making sure everything we do improves patient experience, outcomes, and cost."

Board Compact: Foundation for a Robust Governance Evaluation System

In an effort to help other medical center boards learn from the Virginia Mason experience, Orlikoff and Kaplan authored an article in the journal *Trustee*, a publication aimed at members of nonprofit boards (September 2012). They focused on the value of Virginia Mason's Board Compact—modeled on the original physician compact created in 2001. They write that "most health care systems have implicit, unspoken agreements between and among the organization and its various leadership and caregiver groups." Yet they argue that "most of these tacit compacts are based on economic, social and political relationships and systems that are mired in a distant past and that hinder leaders from effectively moving their organizations into the future." Thus, a new approach is urgently needed: "a new, explicit compact and the process that leads to it" are needed to meet the increasingly challenging demands of provider organizations. Orlikoff and Kaplan note that a Board Compact is analogous to the types of Physician Compacts Virginia Mason established in 2001 and that increasing numbers of organizations have created in recent years.

When the board decided to create a compact, its members examined the "implicit Board Compact," which included such common and outdated concepts as:

1. The primary job of the board was to hire and fire the CEO.
2. The primary obligation of board members was to come to meetings.
3. There was no governance accountability.
4. Board membership was largely honorary.
5. Quality was the job of the doctors and not the board.

In short, the old, tacit governance compact not only was of no value to the vision and journey to which Virginia Mason had committed but also would likely inhibit them.

The Board Compact guides the board in all of its work. It is included in board member packets for every meeting, and, significantly, it is an important element in recruiting new board members. Individuals whose image of a medical center board position leans toward a sense of social connection and influence may be surprised by the Virginia Mason compact. Orlikoff and Kaplan write that the compact

> shows that the organization and the board require of all board members a significant commitment of time and effort... This, in turn, attracts serious, dedicated people to the board and drives the board toward continuous governance improvement. Potential board recruits who might be put off by the compact or disagree with the approach to governance outlined within would have been ineffective members of the board team. Thus, the compact helps VM recruit board members who are in sync with our approach to governance and selects out those who are not.

The compact is also essential to evaluating the performance of each board member through an evaluation system that includes:

- Postboard meeting evaluations after every meeting.
- Annual full board self-evaluations.
- Individual board member performance evaluations pursuant to term renewal.
- Board chair performance evaluations pursuant to term renewal.
- Chair-elect evaluations prior to electing the board chair.

The compact also forms the basis for a key cultural component of Virginia Mason and its governance: the commitment to lean and the Virginia Mason Production System, ensuring that this commitment is "baked into" the board and will survive the departure of any individual executive or board member.

Looking back on the Virginia Mason journey since 2001, it is clear that the board has played a pivotal role all along the way, particularly at crucial moments where courage and vision were required. Never has the board flinched in challenging times. Never have board members been anything but determined to forge ahead with the Virginia Mason Production System. This is a crucial point. The management method, deeply embedded within Virginia Mason, is intended to be sustained for many decades to come. There is no VMPS expiration date, and the board's commitment to maintaining the management method is one of the great essential strengths of the organization. On many occasions, as the board has discussed succession planning, its members have been resolute in their commitment to sustain the Virginia Mason Production System well beyond the tenure of the current leadership team.

And now, on top of that, the board is showing the way for a new and clearly more robust form of governance for health care organizations. Just as VMPS has become a model for so many provider organizations, so too may the form of Virginia Mason governance become a model as well.

Chapter **8**

The Virginia Mason Institute
Leading the Vision to Transform Health Care

Dr. Craig Grimes: Frazzled, Overwhelmed, Skeptical

Dr. Craig Grimes was fed up. He had realized his dream of becoming a medical doctor, and now, after a dozen years of practice, he was frazzled, overwhelmed, on the verge of burnout—and just 41 years old. "I was at a stage of my career where I was completely overwhelmed," he recalls. "I had a very fast growing, busy practice and had just come off a time when I had been overwhelmed by hospital work when we were still doing hospital work. Every night I was bringing hours of work home. I'd work all day, get home and have dinner, put the kids to bed, and work until I went to bed."

In spring 2009, his practice, the North Shore Physicians Group (NSPG), retained the Virginia Mason Institute to teach flow in ambulatory care. Grimes was signed up for the course, but before it started he assumed it would be nonsense. "I was very, very skeptical of the training," he recalls. "I was suspicious of it mainly out of a typical defensive reaction against change, which we see a lot in medicine. A group of our docs had gone to Seattle to look at the program and brought it back to us, but I was suspicious of the fact that there was a movement to standardize work. I just didn't feel medicine could be standardized."

The workshop was led by Dr. Henry Otero from the Virginia Mason Institute and focused on flow in primary care. It was detailed and specific, but the essential point of the training was that the burden of work on physicians could be shifted to other highly competent members of the primary care team—to the benefit of the physician, the other primary care team members, and, most importantly, the patient. The work at Virginia Mason had demonstrated that the flow model enabled doctors to focus more on complex cases while medical assistants, nurses, receptionists, clinical pharmacists, and others picked up various pieces of the work the physician had been doing. The result was much better flow through the clinic and thus more effective use of the doctor's time with patients. It also resulted in improved job satisfaction for medical assistants, nurses, and other team members as well as for doctors. And patient satisfaction scores climbed. On top of it all, because the day's work was done in flow rather than batched (that pile of work Grimes had been bringing home), Virginia Mason physicians completed their work soon after their last appointment of the day.

While Otero and Grimes were talking early in the training, Otero said that working in flow prevented a wide variety of mistakes. When not in flow, he explained, crucial patient information such as blood work can get lost in the shuffle, even delayed for days. Otero knew of cases where a potentially life-threatening potassium level of 8.0 was missed by doctors not in flow. Grimes was taken aback. "That happened to me," he told Otero. "That happened to me this weekend. On Sunday. I left here Friday with a full pile of labs on my desk and came in Sunday night and went through the list," and there was a patient with a dangerous potassium level.

Grimes called the patient's home right away, and his wife answered. Her husband had felt very ill and was rushed to the hospital where he was in the ICU. "At that point Craig knew that his process had jeopardized quality and safety," says Otero. Flow training had a profound impact on Grimes. He says:

> I came out of the four-day workshop and felt completely transformed. There was something that happened during that ambulatory flow workshop, some moment, where I realized that my

professional life does not have to be the way it is now, and if I change the way I perceive work throughout the day and eliminate batching I'll be able to keep up with my work. The second to the last day of the workshop Henry came to my office and rearranged it and got a flow station put up. Henry was really my mentor through all of this. I went home that night and took all my extra work with me and caught up overnight, and that was the last time I really had to bring work home. That was October 2010.

When You Look at Your Practice from a Population Standpoint You See It Differently

Grimes works under an internal performance framework requiring physicians to hit certain clinical quality benchmarks to receive funds withheld from their pay. For the past two years, since he has been both in flow in the clinic and able to focus more energy to population health management, Grimes has been able to achieve difficult performance goals:

> You cannot do population health management in batch work. That is an essential lesson of the Virginia Mason approach—that batching work is inherently wasteful. With the population health management you have to do a little bit every day to ensure you are communicating effectively with patients. We have our lists of patients who aren't achieving their goals at any given time and we really work on that.
>
> Part of the reason I like this and do well in it is because I have come to the belief that when you look at your practice from a population standpoint you see it differently. We think about individual patients in exam rooms and we tell ourselves we do the right thing every time, but when you look at results over the population you see that you don't. You need to see results in the aggregate.

Everything Gary Said Resonated with Me

Partners HealthCare is one of the most prestigious health care organizations in the world. Its two signature medical centers— Massachusetts General and Brigham & Women's Hospital—are renowned globally. Not only is Partners the dominant player in the Greater Boston marketplace, but it is also the largest employer in Massachusetts. All of this raises an obvious question: How did the North Shore Physicians Group, an integral part of the Partners behemoth, decide to revamp its delivery system based on work pioneered by a mid-sized medical center in Seattle, Washington?

It started in 2009 when Steve Kapfhammer listened to Gary Kaplan speak. Kapfhammer is president of the North Shore Physicians Group, and as he sat in the audience at the Group Practice Improvement Network (GPIN) gathering, he realized that "everything Gary said resonated with me. He focused on measurable, positive outcomes on quality, safety, and efficiency and he was able to demonstrate how the key measures were improving including patient and employee satisfaction and his bottom line margin."

"Our physicians were very siloed in 11 different locations throughout the North Shore area of Boston," he says. "There was no overarching strategy among the locations and no group culture." This was a significant problem particularly in light of the rapid-fire changes spreading throughout the health care world. Kapfhammer knew that in this period of turmoil and change that a siloed group lacking cultural alignment was playing with fire. Kapfhammer was working to align the strategy and culture throughout all of his practice sites, and he had a sense after hearing Kaplan that the Virginia Mason approach might help.

Fortuitously, soon after hearing Kaplan speak, Kapfhammer attended a North Shore Medical Center senior leadership retreat where one of the assigned readings happened to be a Harvard Business School case study on Virginia Mason. On top of that, at the same time, GPIN offered its members, including Kapfhammer's group, slots in a Virginia Mason workshop focused on flow in ambulatory care. In spring 2010, three doctors and a manager from North Shore Physicians Group travelled to Seattle for the workshop. Otero hosted the group in Seattle:

> The providers who come here to see what we do are typically over-burdened with poor quality, poor work–life balance, patients not satisfied with the clinic experience and on and on. We try and help them see a different way of doing things; a different future

in health care. We try and teach and show them things that are answers to the problems they face; that will mean better quality for their patients.

I explain that the lean methods and process are the start of a journey. "It doesn't have to be this way the rest of your life." We showed them the clinics here at General Internal Medicine—Virginia Mason's largest primary care site in downtown Seattle, a location formerly characterized by chaos and dysfunction, now running so smoothly the waiting rooms were nearly empty even though every provider's schedule was full.

Watching them you could see the light bulb go on. They could see the promise this had for his organization. That's the spark we are always trying to start with. For people to be open and see new ways and realize, "I can change the future!"

The NSPG team returned home on fire, says Kapfhammer. They saw that using the Virginia Mason approach it was possible to get today's work done today—to leave the office without a batch of work to do at home. However enthusiastic some leaders might be, it is important to engage physician leaders in the work, particularly those who might initially express a degree of skepticism. Dr. Maury McGough, medical director of NSPG, was just such a skeptic. "When I started the training, my initial response was, 'I know how to practice medicine. I have been doing this for 20 years with a very large patient panel and doing it well. This does not apply to me; it applies to younger doctors.' But on the first day of training I realized how wrong I was. It was showing me the power of flow—showing how much more efficient you can be if you do things in flow. It woke me up to the burden of work I didn't need to be doing."

About five months after her flow training, McGough was away skiing:

Usually skiing for the weekend for me meant I would go out and ski for three hours, leave the family out there, and come back to the house to work on my charts. I would sneak time every ski weekend to get caught up. This particular weekend I came in from skiing, and there was nothing in my inbox. I thought, "*What happened last week? Did I work late? Why* am I caught up for the first time in 25 years?" And the answer is that I was gradually bringing flow into my day-to-day life, and all of my team members were taking on a good part of the work I used to do. They had slowly taught me how to let them do that. It makes it a more rewarding place for everybody to work because everybody is empowered to make it better.

Reflecting upon the work, McGough says that the Virginia Mason approach to "creating a really safe environment for our patients and decreasing the burden of work for our care givers are messages that resonate beautifully with everybody who chooses to work in the business of life which is what we've done. It is a much more powerful message than 'we are going to take out waste.'"

The initial phase of the work North Shore Physicians Group did with Virginia Mason went so well that Kapfhammer and his colleagues wanted more. They believed that adapting a full measure of the Virginia Mason approach would enable the organization to get to its quality goals much faster. Thus, in spring 2011 the group entered into an agreement to provide training and education services. Since that time a number of institute personnel have worked with the group but the mainstays have been Otero and Chris Backous.

"Chris and Henry really resonate with us," says Kapfhammer. "Henry with the doctors and Chris with our staff." "They were interested in the management system, not just the tools—a critical distinction," says Otero. "What has made NSPG successful has been the tremendous commitment of their leadership. They have a vision for patient care and they are looking for a method to achieve that and they really see how the VMPS structure allows them to get there. They have a relentless pursuit of patient-first care and quality. That constancy of purpose helps them get through the hard times of adopting this method."

It Was a Life-Changing Experience

While the North Shore Physicians Group was deeply engaged with the Virginia Mason approach, their umbrella organization— North Shore Medical Center—was pursuing other improvement efforts. "I watched the physician group's journey in parallel with the hospital journey," says Bob Norton, CEO of the medical center. "We had a much more eclectic approach at the hospital."

But the question was whether two distinctly different improvement approaches—one for the physician's group and another for the hospital—made any sense? "We had a good deal of debate in the hospital about whether a common methodology could help us reach our improvement goals more quickly," says Norton. "There was not a total consensus but more people thought so than didn't." Norton and his hospital leadership team engaged in discussions with the institute, and one of the suggestions Otero and Diane Miller made was for Norton, Kapfhammer, and their colleagues to join a delegation of Virginia Mason executives in their annual pilgrimage to Japan.

The Japan trip was a treasured Virginia Mason tradition. When Kaplan led the first pilgrimage to Japan in spring 2002, he brought along the top 30 leaders within the organization. Many people—doctors and administrators back at Virginia Mason and certainly his competitors in Seattle—thought what he was doing was absurd. Yet every year Kaplan had returned, leading teams to various factories of Japanese firms to deepen their understanding and hone their skills. Over the years, the essence of the Toyota Production System attached itself to the Virginia Mason DNA. The trip was revered by those who had been on it. Yet all veterans said it was a grueling, exhausting affair. The question for Bob Norton, after nearly four decades in health care, was this: Would he travel nearly 7,000 miles to work in a Hitachi air conditioning plant to learn how to improve quality at his hospital and physician group on Boston's North Shore?

Norton went all in. At Hitachi, he and his colleagues were part of teams that worked on the production line with the goal of reducing waste and identifying improvements in their process. Says Norton:

We were seeing the science of the Toyota Production System applied to a vastly different production line from health care, but we were seeing that the principles and concepts are exactly the same. It opened everybody's eyes. There is this myth we have been living under that our business is totally different than all other businesses but we could see that it was just that, a myth.

There is something about seeing it in action, really seeing it in action in the presence of a language barrier that forces you to look for universality. It was a life-changing experience. It was one of the most interesting things I have done in my 37 years in this business. We were benefiting both from the expertise of the Virginia Mason folks and from the expertise of lean trained leaders at a Hitachi factory.

Dr. Mitch Rein, chief medical officer for North Shore Medical Center, had a similar reaction to the Japan trip. "It was life-changing for me on so many levels," he says. "Part of it is what we learned from our colleagues on the trip—the Virginia Mason staff and part of it was what we learned from people at Toyota and Hitachi. It was so inspirational and energizing to see them build systems and support resiliency and joy in work. I've gone to a lot of meetings over the years and come back from some a little bit pumped, but *nothing* like what I experienced on the trip to Japan."

The Lean Tools and Virginia Mason Principles Resonate Extremely Well Here

Norton gave two reasons for deciding to extend the lean work from the physician group to the hospital. First, he believed it would accelerate the pace of change and improvement, and, second, "a driving factor was the blurring of lines around inpatient and outpatient and population health management requiring us to look across those lines in a way we never have before. The only way to do it is to manage a life as opposed to a particular admission." Each time the lean management approach breaks through in an organization, it seems to make its reception at least a bit smoother in other organizations particularly when they are linked, as the North Shore hospital and physician group are. "There's been some healthy skepticism in the hospital," says Norton. "But the doctors on the hospital side saw the success the docs on the physician group side were having and when you see real results there's less skepticism. It is a great opportunity for us in the hospital to move into this world preceded by the pioneering work the physician practice did."

Rein says the accelerating pace of change in health care makes the Virginia Mason approach particularly valuable. "The lean tools and Virginia Mason principles resonate extremely well here and are preparing us for an enormous amount of change," he says, and those tools and principles "help our focus on improvement, care redesign and patient affordability as our lead strategy." During his career, Rein has "been involved in a number of different improvement frameworks, and to me this is a framework that has the highest probability" to achieve three important goals starting with improving the quality of care. Second, he says, is "to improve the value of care and the immense pressure we have on patient affordability." And third is the impact the approach can have on the lives of caregivers. "This approach puts an enormous amount of focus on decreasing the burden of work and improving the work environment for my physician and nursing colleagues," he says. "It uses simple methods to remove waste, standardize the work, and decrease the burden of work for our providers."

The turbulence and accelerating rate of change in health care make change and improvement particularly challenging. It is in times such as these that the question of what leadership looks like takes on particular relevance. Consider the situation faced by the leadership team (Norton, Kapfhammer, McGough, Rein, and their colleagues) on the North Shore. They are gearing up for the shift from a homegrown electronic health care record to an Epic system in 2016—a shift that is nearly always disruptive. They are working on the patient-centered medical home, and there are, of course, the daily needs of the organization—the need to see thousands of patients. None of this, as Kapfhammer likes to point out, constitutes low-hanging fruit.

And there remains some questioning about the Virginia Mason methods even as the calendar in both the physician's group and the hospital fill with kaizen events that require staff members to be taken off line for a day, a few days, a week, to work on improvement. Notwithstanding all of this, Norton and Kapfhammer and their colleagues in leadership are forging ahead convinced this approach will provide the best route to superb patient-centered care. "We are really, really putting the patient in the center, and that's why we went to medical school," says Rein. "It's where the professional joy and gratitude come from."

Otero is impressed with the progress the North Shore group has made. "They have demonstrated success in their engagement of the physician group in this process and improvement method," he says. "They have made gains in patient experience of care and it is helping them meet the cost–quality challenge."

Can We Really Do What Virginia Mason Has Done?

What became known as the Virginia Mason Institute had modest roots in the early days of Virginia Mason's adaptation of the Toyota Production System to health care. A few early articles in the press, including a mention in the *Wall Street Journal* in 2004, brought early visitors who were curious as much as anything. After Virginia Mason was on this course for just two years, word got out throughout the health care community in the United States that this highly unusual experiment was taking place: "They are doing *what*? Using Toyota's manufacturing methods in a medical center? But people aren't cars!"

It sounded preposterous to many people in health care. However, early results gained some positive publicity, and as soon as that happened clinicians and administrators were on the phone asking whether they could come see the work in action. All were welcome, yet over time the number of visitors grew to the point where it was an intrusion on the work. It was clear that a new entity was needed to respond to the mounting demand for teaching and coaching—thus was born the Virginia Mason Institute in 2009. Its mission was to teach, of course, but it was also a tangible manifestation of Virginia Mason's commitment to follow through on its promise and vision within the Strategic Plan to transform health care.

Two assumptions lie at the heart of this mission. First, countless organizations are seeking a new pathway forward as they realize that the current turmoil demands a new way of delivering care. The second assumption upon which the mission rests is that the Virginia Mason approach is strong enough to transform health care and that the Virginia Mason teams have the ability to fan out across the country and teach its method well enough so that other organizations are able to adapt it and achieve results comparable to what Virginia Mason has achieved.

And while many health care leaders out there are stuck in the status quo, unwilling or unable to innovate, many others are actively looking for a way to bet the farm on quality. And as these leaders look around for a methodology to carry them forward, increasing numbers are finding that lean management promises significant gains. It is at this juncture that many leaders find themselves on a plane to Seattle. Some arrive at Virginia Mason to window-shop. They are interested in an overview of the methodology and tools, and then they need time to go back home and mull it over. Others have dipped their toe into lean but came away with a less than optimal experience, often involving pushback and resistance from within their own organization. They seek to understand where they might have made a misstep and how they might restart the lean engine. And then there are organizations that come ready to change and having done enough background study that they feel a certain confidence that the Virginia Mason Production System is right for them.

Diane Miller serves as both executive director of the institute as well as vice president of Virginia Mason Medical Center. Diane has earned VMPS certification and has extensive training in applying the Toyota Production System to health care, including more than one study mission to Japan to the shingijutsu genba kaizen. She has led many rapid process improvement workshops and has developed health care curriculum for the training of leaders and staff. Miller built a small staff in the early days of the institute and designed training programs to serve the needs of what would soon become a large customer base for the institute. From the start in October 2008, the institute was created as a tax exempt nonprofit education and training organization. Says Miller:

> We felt the institute was a way to fulfill our obligation to help transform health care and at the same time recoup some of our own investment to reinvest in our own continued learning. Over the years as there is more and more evidence that this approach does work, we've had steady increases in people coming to us to learn and to coach them through their change process. People ask: what will it take to get the kind of results you get? In some cases

the CEO comes and is trying to figure out whether this is the right approach. In other cases there are leaders within an organization convinced this is the route to go, but they need more information and evidence to win over their leadership.

Initially, the institute offered one-day seminars to build awareness and understanding of the Virginia Mason Production System. Soon thereafter, skill development workshops were offered. Over time, Miller and her colleagues developed more advanced training for those interested in building their technical skills. Popular courses in lean training and advanced lean training are targeted largely for middle managers wishing to develop expertise and perhaps work in a kaizen promotion office.

When the institute was up and running in 2009, Virgin Mason had a solid 7 years of experience using the Virginia Mason Production System. As a result, the teams had scores of metrics and case studies that demonstrated the impact of the methodology on efficiency, safety, quality, patient experience, and cost. Visitors saw that the indicators were moving in a positive direction. "They want to understand as executives how they need to change to lead in a different way," says Miller. "Most of the leaders who come for a visit realize very quickly how strong the alignment is on our strategic direction and, although when asked they all say they have Strategic Plans, they are all pretty unanimous in saying that those plans are not living and breathing the strategy at the front lines."

Miller and her colleagues at the institute emphasize that the kind of transformation Virginia Mason has experienced can happen only if it is led from the top of the organization. "It does require senior executives to change first," she says. "This is not a middle management delegated activity to transform an organization and culture." The ultimate question many clinicians and administrators ask when they learn about the Virginia Mason work is, "Can we really do what they have done?" Miller has a ready answer: "*Of course* you can do it! The principles are the principles. It's about really aligning yourself with those teachings from Deming and Toyota applied with rigor."

Chief operating officer Sarah Patterson stresses the point about leadership:

If leaders aren't all in, this won't work. We have people ask us, 'Don't we need a Gary Kaplan to pull this off?' And the answer is that you need *leaders*. They won't all look or be just like Gary, but if they are effective leaders they will be able to do this. Sometimes people who visit us—department or section heads—say their CEO isn't interested in this and they wonder whether they should go ahead and try to implement it in their department? That isn't ideal, but if they can demonstrate results to their CEO maybe the work can spread to other areas.

You could start a model line or pilot in one part of the organization to prove the concept to the skeptics, but I always try and make clear that the power of VMPS comes with every part of the organization working to support the value streams. That is why you need the entire organization involved.

Miller cautions that Virginia Mason's experience demonstrates that early coaching is essential. John Black, a lean consultant and former Boeing executive, helped guide Virginia Mason through the first few years of its experience and that guidance was critically important. "The answer is absolutely you can do this, but you can't do it without an outside coach," she says. "You need somebody you can trust because it becomes a partnership—a coach who both coaches and challenges. It is so easy inside an organization to rely on old approaches, and there is always organizational politics to contend with. It is very easy to not see what you need to see as the reality of the current state." Creating flow in the ambulatory setting is the single most popular institute program. With widespread angst and dysfunction throughout the world of primary care, clinicians seem amazed to find a methodology that is fairly easily adaptable and helps solve many of the problems that plague large numbers of practices. The training includes physicians, practice managers, and medical assistants who serve as flow managers. Once trained, teams are quickly able to incorporate many of the changes at home.

The institute offers a wide variety of seminars and training from a basic introduction to full-scale partnership where institute personnel work on a transformation initiative in partnership with an organization. "We've seen a shift to more organizations who are interested in developing their own capability, so we coach them on that," says Miller. "Reliance on others for training is not a long term strategy." Ultimately, the challenge for any organization seeking to learn from Virginia Mason comes down to culture. A lean management method along with lean tools can be profoundly effective within an organization whose culture has evolved to the point where learning, experimentation and the constant search for improvement is welcome. The Virginia Mason way is not mechanical; it's in the bones, in the heart, and—if all goes well for a time—finds its way into an organization's DNA. The most profound transformation at Virginia Mason is not about a methodology or tools. It is about a fundamentally different culture.

Doctors Were Unhappy and Revenues Were Down

Four hundred and fifty miles to the southwest of the North Shore Medical Center lies Summit Health, the dominant provider in Franklin County, Pennsylvania. Summit is centered in the southern portion of the state near the Maryland border. It sits 160 miles west of Philadelphia and about 85 miles from Baltimore. Summit Health includes two hospitals, one in Chambersburg and the other in Waynesboro, and approximately 25 clinical locations spread throughout Franklin County. There are many differences between the North Shore group and Summit, but both share a deep desire to apply lean methods and tools to provide more efficient, safer, higher-quality, and more affordable care to their patients.

The germ of the lean idea at Summit originated at Summit with Niki Showe, vice president for physician practices, when she looked around and saw that the doctors were unhappy and revenues were down. "The financial losses were increasing all the time and there was real concern about it," she says. "The doctors were saying they were overwhelmed, some were burned out, and they were all saying that they were not getting enough time to take care of patients. Doctors talked about how miserable they were coming to work." Showe could see that the burden on the physicians was unreasonable, and she also believed it was eminently fixable. The issue, from her standpoint, was that too much work that could be handled by others in primary care was on the shoulders of the doctors.

There was something odd about this. Summit teams had previously distributed a good deal of work from primary care physicians to others on the team as a way to reduce the burden of work on doctors and enable them to focus more on patients. "We had gone from having medical assistants and nurses do more of the work to doctors basically doing everything," she says. "It happened because there had been a faulty theory as we implemented our electronic medical record that we had many staff members doing work physicians were ultimately responsible for. So instead of keeping work with less expensive staff resources it was decided to put it on the doctors shoulders." This move, which resulted in layoffs to a number of clinical staff, backfired. Showe found herself facing a perfect storm of unhappy physicians and declining revenues. She realized that it was essential to shift the work distribution back to where it had been with various clinical staff members taking shares of physicians' duties.

Showe also had basic knowledge of lean management from study and reading she had done several years earlier. At that time she had also visited JLG Industries, Inc., in nearby McConnellsburg, Pennsylvania. JLG is a global manufacturer of aerial work platforms and had integrated lean approaches in some of its work. "Of course it wasn't completely aligned with what we do in health care but it made a lot of sense in streamlining work and cutting duplication," she says. Someone from JLG had explained to her that the company shifted some work from highly paid engineers to other staff members to make sure the engineers were focused on work only they were capable of handling. Showe liked the obvious comparison to Summit and reasoned that a lean management approach might work there.

She spoke with Pat O'Donnell, then the Summit chief financial officer (since promoted to CEO), and he encouraged her efforts. She looked at some work the University of Michigan had done in lean applications to health care, and, at O'Donnell's urging, she wrote a proposal to the Summit Endowment Fund. She felt she had made a strong case for how lean management in primary care would benefit doctors, patients and thus, the community as a whole, but she was turned down.

But several years later the time was right. During a retreat for senior management, one of her colleagues, a physician leader, mentioned the possibility of integrating lean management at Summit. Showe was already familiar with the health care organizations best known for their adoption of lean, and her first call went to the Virginia Mason Institute.

In May 2012, soon after talking with Otero, Showe and Dr. Frank Mozdy from Summit traveled to Seattle for a workshop focused on flow in ambulatory care. They visited Virginia Mason's largest primary care site in downtown Seattle. The team at the clinic answered many questions from Showe and Mozdy about how they might shift the balance of work so that it could be more evenly spread among various primary care team members.

Showe and Mozdy spoke with Dr. Kim Pittenger from another Virginia Mason clinic and were struck by the sense of energy and excitement Pittenger felt about the flow process. He made clear that it had significantly reduced the burden of work on physicians, elevated various other member of the primary care team resulting in better care, improved patient experience, and higher job satisfaction scores for doctors as well as medical assistants and others. "They were really clear and helpful on how we could help the doctors so they could focus on patients and not get burned out," Showe says.

Showe and Mozdy were sufficiently energized by their Seattle visit that they asked Otero to come to Chambersburg to present the flow workshop to a large number of physicians and staff at Summit. In the meantime, Showe made sure all the senior executives at Summit Physicians Services as well as members of the board received copies of the book *Transforming Health Care: Virginia Mason Medical Center's Pursuit of the Perfect Patient Experience* (Productivity Press, 2011). "It helped make sense of the lean approach for our board members," says Showe, "but most of our doctors had a hard time believing it could be that good." Showe and Mozdy wanted to use the lean management system to transform the way work was done and care delivered at Summit Physician Services. They aspired to a changed culture with the patient first in everything at all times, with a patient-centered medical home with doctors and other clinicians working in teams, with a widespread respect among all colleagues for patients as well as one another, with a deep passion for safety as the first commitment to patients at all times, and with far less waste and greater efficiency.

"Niki and I told Henry," says Mozdy. "We didn't just want to learn how to use a tool we wanted to make this the way we do work. We had been putting out fires in the physician group and using bandaids, and we knew we needed to do something much more substantial and sustainable. During the ambulatory flow workshop Niki and I were taking notes all the time thinking about ways we could apply the approach at Summit and which of our docs would like it. Our heads were swimming with all these possibilities. We sat down with Henry after the workshop and said we definitely want to do full transformation. We don't want to just dabble in it."

But before Summit committed to a broad contract with the Virginia Mason Institute, Showe knew it was necessary to conduct more due diligence. She returned to Seattle in late 2012 for a couple of reasons. She wanted Pat O'Donnell, who would soon be CEO, to see the Virginia Mason teams in action. Also joining Showe and O'Donnell on the trip were Mozdy and Lorentsen as well as several other senior leaders from Summit Physician services. In addition to exposing O'Donnell to Virginia Mason, she wanted to kick the tires one more time to make sure she had done an effective job of due diligence. Showe and her colleagues probed, asking questions of the Virginia Mason team members, seeing whether any of them would confide that they were actually not so enamored of the lean methodology; maybe that it wasn't all that it was cracked up to be. "But there was nothing even remotely like that," says Showe. "Every single person we talked with there really believed in the approach and everybody seemed so engaged and excited about the work. It was an amazing alignment."

During the course of the trip Showe said that they could see in action much of what had been written in the book *Transforming Health Care*. "We talked with the people who were written about in the book and everything we read about we could see some part of it firsthand," she says. The Summit team met with Kaplan. "Gary told us about how when Virginia Mason started its journey people said that it couldn't be done, that you could not adapt the Toyota Production System to health care. He said there were a lot of naysayers at the start but that many of those naysayers were now among the strongest believers in the approach. Gary really inspired us and when we flew home there was a lot of new energy. On the red eye flight home I sat with Pat and we stayed awake the whole night and just talked about it." Embracing a new management method would present Summit Physician Services with enormous challenges, and while Showe and Mozdy were enthusiastic, it would require robust support from the entire leadership team to proceed. During a gathering of the 15 or so senior leaders, Showe and Mozdy made their position clear. "Then we said to the rest of the group, 'Are you going to be behind this or not?' And everybody in senior management said, 'Yes, this is the way we need to go.'"

After entering into a transformation contract with the Virginia Mason Institute Mozdy and Showe asked Otero to speak to the Summit board of directors and hospital leaders as well. "We were feeling like we couldn't tell enough people at that point—we wanted people to know how exciting this could be." But Showe knew Summit's culture well, and she knew to proceed with a certain degree of caution. "Not everyone is going to be on board right away," she says. "We started experimenting with the people who had some enthusiasm." She would nudge, but not too forcefully. "Let's just try it," she told clinical teams. "If you are not comfortable yet, it's okay."

In February 2013, Showe, along with Mozdy, Bea Hoffman, and James Pryor, returned to Seattle for training to become certified lean trainers, which would enable them to lead improvement events including rapid process improvement workshops. Initially, the training can be somewhat overwhelming. These are very busy people who have now taken on a week of training in addition to an assignment back home to work on a specific improvement project then return to Seattle a month later for additional training. "Henry told me to make sure I set aside 50 percent of my time to work on the improvement project; I didn't do it, and I wasn't able to finish my assignment until the day we arrived in Seattle." Otero started regular monthly visits to Summit in spring 2013, and he has seen the teams there make steady progress since then.

One of the most impactful RPIWs focused on safety. The RPIW team included all of the clinicians involved as well as a patient who had received a disabling hospital-acquired infection. The damage to the patient had been so severe that he has been trying to recuperate for 6 years. At one time his daughter had to move in to care for him. He lost huge amounts of income from missing work. He has been a long-term patient in the wound care center. "It was our fault," says Showe, and to acknowledge and face that reality—with the patient right there as part of the RPIW team—was immensely powerful. During the RPIW it became clear that most employees at Summit did not understand how to properly and safely move a patient. The result has been widespread retraining throughout the organization to ensure employees understand the safest ways to move a patient to insure that bed sores and other potential infections do not occur. After the RPIW, O'Donnell declared that Summit's number-one priority going forward would be safety. He told a gathering of employees that it was no longer an expectation that employees would report potential patient harm: "it is your responsibility to do so."

We Learned an Important Lesson, and There Were a Lot of Hurt Feelings

During training for flow in ambulatory care, Lorentsen had an aha moment on the second day. He and Stine were going through one of the exercises, and there was some discussion about Summit adopting the flow stations in six months or so. "And Kristi said to me, 'Why don't you do this right away?' But I resisted that. Summit is not like that or certainly was not like that. I have been here 18 years and Summit has always been very stiff. There is not a lot of physician leadership. We would get directives from senior management and they would tell us how to practice. Any time we wanted to change something it was painfully slow and there was a lot of resistance." On the third day of the workshop Lorentsen asked Stine whether she really thought they would able to implement the flow process, and she said she definitely believed they could. They decided to take the plunge. The following week Stine explained to the three other doctors working in Lorentsen's practice what the flow concept was all about and how it worked at Virginia Mason and could work at Summit.

They implemented the flow process and station virtually overnight. It made for much better communication between the two of them. After a morning huddle to prepare for the day the new approach allowed Lorentsen to move rapidly through the work of the day with Stine taking increasing responsibility for handling non visit work, thus reducing the burden of work on Lorentsen and allowing him to focus on the patients in front of him. The approach, says Lorentsen, brought him closer to patients. He never used to answer the telephone, for example, but now does so often because so much of the other administrative work is off his shoulders. "The whole idea of not batching work and dealing with things as they come up right away was so effective," he says. "Getting work done in flow meant we had more time for patients and patients feel they have a lot more access."

But something went awry. In their eagerness to establish flow in their practice, Lorentsen and Stine missed a key step: they failed to till the soil, as the Japanese say, to prepare others with whom they worked for the change. They made the change. It worked for them. And they moved on. But this approach nearly always creates confusion and resentment among team members. "We got feedback that what we were doing was interfering with teamwork and that there was less esprit de corps among the three other docs and our staff members," says Lorentsen. "We got a comment from another nurse that we used to be team under the old system and now Stine working as flow manager was not helping the team. And there is a whole vocabulary that goes along with lean principles and tools, and we started using that vocabulary and it irritated some of the staff. It was as though there was this secret lingo, and that made people uncomfortable."

Showe added, "We learned an important lesson—that we needed to choose our process owners and sponsors carefully. Dr. Lorentsen was process owner but didn't have direct responsibility for what they we were changing. At the same time the office manager and others were preparing for go-live for a new oncology computer, and the office manager was not available for the RPIW. Dr. Lorentsen wanted to move forward. But the person responsible for how the office was managed was not on the team. There were a lot of hurt feelings."

By spring 2014 Summit had momentum. All senior managers were on a path toward certification, and there was minimal resistance within the organization to the new direction perhaps because "we keep doing it at slow and steady pace," says Pryor. "We knew at the start that if we commit to this it has to become our philosophy, our way of life and we are all in. We are going to be together for the good and the bad and ugly. We are there for each other. It really fit with what we were doing trying to get docs more in leadership—more doctors at the table helping steer us in better direction. We bring validity to the process for doctors because it is science based."

With VMPS We Can Do So Much More for Patients

The mission to transform health care demands that the institute show tangible results that what Virginia Mason has done can be replicated. North Shore and Summit are among scores of organizations serving as living proof that the lean methods work and that proof attracts greater numbers to the lean pathway. "We need to continue to demonstrate that the structure and methods we use at Virginia Mason can work in any health care organization as long as leadership is committed to the methodology, and they recognize that it is a journey," says Otero. "Part of the Institute's goal is to expose more people to understanding the methodology as it applies to health care. We want to create excitement and engagement around this method to show people they can create a different future for themselves and their organizations." Miller says that she sees a trend where the institute will bring more and more services to organizations to guide their transformation journeys. "We will also have more on site services and will expand our virtual learning experiences. And there is a considerable demand from overseas."

The Virginia Mason Institute has a critical role in achieving the mission of transforming health care through inspiring and showing a new way health care can be. Miller and Otero say that it is essential the institute extend its reach farther upstream in educational programs. This means integrating the institute curriculum—or something very much like it—into master's programs, nursing programs, and medical schools. To this end, Otero's role is shifting from consulting in the field to focusing on developing curricula that can be spread and adopted at various educational levels.

Miller and Otero have made a start toward this teaching at the University Of Washington School of Public Health. In a course called process quality management, they teach the fundamentals of lean management as it applies to health care. They use Virginia Mason as a case study, and the students do their own observations, value stream maps, and propose kaizen activity for their final projects. For Otero, the shift from working as a medical oncologist for 12 years to serving in a leadership role at the institute has broadened his horizons. "My mission as a physician started with working to change the life of the person in front of me," he says. And through the years he worked as a medical oncologist at Virginia Mason he felt a great sense of satisfaction at helping hundreds of sick patients—some very sick patients:

> But to me being a good doctor wasn't enough and isn't enough to insure that the person sitting across from me is going to get great care. With VMPS we can do so much more for patients than I can provide to a person sitting across from me in the exam room. Fixing the process by which care is delivered can have a much bigger impact. There is a bigger crisis out there, and going from helping a limited number of people in my oncology practice to making organizations aware of how to approach health care delivery in a different way—that is much more impactful on people's health and outcomes.

Chapter 9

Virginia Mason's Essential Elements

It started out as a casual exercise. I asked one of the Virginia Mason executives what she considered the essential elements of the organization's success. "Alignment, teamwork, and transparency," she said, without hesitating. She thought for an additional moment before adding, "And definitely accountability—and we are, maybe as much as anything, a learning organization."

What would happen, I wondered, if I asked a couple of dozen executive leaders the same question? How much alignment would there be? The next person I asked gave me exactly the same list as the first person, but he added humility and optimism. Someone else added courage and urgency. And so it went as I posed the same question again and again to the leadership team—the same responses kept coming back. The consistency seemed both proof of alignment and emblematic of the culture. Over time so many thoughtful comments came on these essential elements that I decided to get out of the way and gather the quotes by category. I think they speak volumes. Here are the voices of a number of Virginia Mason leaders on what the executive team clearly sees as the foundational characteristics and attributes upon which Virginia Mason's success has been built.

Optimism
Humility
Alignment
Accountability
Learning organization
Courage
Urgency
Teamwork
Transparency

Optimism

Sarah Patterson is an important guide when it comes to thinking about the overarching characteristics of the organization. Invariably, she starts with the patient's point of view. "Each time we set the targets for a rapid process improvement event," she says, "we need to make a choice to be optimistic because that is what our patients expect. Sometimes event leaders are worried that if we set targets too high for the team then they will be demoralized if they don't achieve them. We always have to ask what would our patients expect from us when we set this target?"

> Health care is not a very optimistic industry today. If you make projections about all the changes, none of them look good. However, I believe at Virginia Mason we have a vision that we can get better. We truly believe we can be the quality leader and transform health care for our patients, and for others. As a result, we have hope. Hope is a good, optimistic feeling to have.
>
> **Sue Anderson**

> Optimism that we can make it different. We have the means and the ability. This also means we have a calling or obligation to make it different. We have demonstrated the difference that can be made, now we need to increase the urgency in getting it changed.
>
> **Charleen Tachibana**

Our sense of optimism comes from the power of this unifying management method we all know and are competent in; the philosophy around reducing waste and being in control of how we do our work. Our optimism is knowing that whatever life throws at us, whatever changes come in health care, we know we have a way to find new solutions in a very rapid way. We have confidence in the method and trust the process.

Diane Miller

I love the Virginia Mason Production System because there are things you can control and things you cannot control. I cannot control the Congress in Washington, D.C., but I can control what is right in front of me. We give patients hope because we have a methodology to do something.

Steve Schaefer

You always see optimism at Friday report-out. You can feel the optimism surface when people talk about what they have discovered in their own areas and how they have improved. That is the one place you hear optimism all the time.

Linda Hebish

Humility

Dr. Bob Caplan vividly recalls the earliest days of the Virginia Mason journey to adapt the Toyota Production System to health care. "Humility was the beginning of our story," he told me. "We started our journey by recognizing that we were not as good as we thought we were. That sense of humility is here with us today in the middle of our journey, and I trust it will be with us always to help us accelerate the pace of learning."

The greatest example of our humility is our willingness to be open to our defects and mistakes, our willingness to talk about it across the system and not point fingers.

Darlene Corkrum

If you come to our meetings you will hear us talking about how we haven't gone far enough. If something isn't improving or if there is a defect, we wonder, "God how could this happen?" We're working at this for 12 years, and I come here every day and see so many things we need to fix. There is so much we have not done.

Dr. Joyce Lammert

The humility of being a learner. Realizing you never fully understand and always learning from others' points of view.

Diane Miller

The more transparent you are the more you realize you are not perfect. That creates great humility. We walk very humbly as long as we remain transparent about our work.

Steve Schaefer

We don't get caught up in our press clippings. We continue to remind ourselves that Toyota has been on this journey for 60-plus years, and that helps you remain humble. We know how important it is for leaders to be humble and listen.

Lynne Chafetz

When I first arrived we had a bigger ego than we do now. Part of that is our transparency and more people within the organization are aware that we still have a ways to go to be the quality leader... We have more humility. We check ourselves a little bit more with humility and the desire to continue to learn.

Katerie Chapman

The ability to realize we are not as good as we think we are. To be humble and learn. It's an element of losing the arrogance; looking for what is not working and focusing on that.

Charleen Tachibana

The biggest room in the "house" is the room for improvement. Never assume you are "here." There is no end line.

Dr. Kim Pittenger

It's important to be a lifelong learner. Too often executives feel the need to know everything; if you know everything then you don't need to learn anything new. Trust that the team can come up with something better than one can do alone. Don't be afraid to say, "I don't know." Humility is being able to do all of this.

Sue Anderson

A leader needs to acknowledge our improvements and accolades but never, ever, settle for status quo. They must routinely remind themselves and share this with their direct reports and colleagues. We are doing great things, and we have a long way to go to reach our vision and deliver on our mission.

Linda Hebish

Humility and learning organization go hand in hand. You're humble in knowing you could always be better and you are always learning. Confidence that comes from using [Virginia Mason Production System] VMPS allows you to know you'll be able to improve it—that you have the means to make things better.

Dr. Donna Smith

Teamwork

Jim Cote has a rather unique perspective having worked at major health care organizations in Boston before joining Virginia Mason. The cultural differences between the East Coast and West Coast in health care are obvious to anyone, like Cote, who has experienced both. What does he see as a defining difference between Virginia Mason and the organizations in which he formerly worked? "What stands out to me having worked in other organizations is the respect for the voice of each team member. When we hold an improvement event teams are made up of people across the organization and from various roles and *every* voice is important and respected."

You won't break down the silos of the different health care professions if the leaders are not role modeling teamwork. When our nursing and pharmacy leaders are aligned on what is the important work and are demonstrating respect for each other, you really start to see true team work between the frontline nurses and pharmacists.

Sarah Patterson

All of health care delivery is moving from the idea of autonomy to teamwork. In our VMPS management method there is a deep understanding and appreciation of the role of every member of the team. We work to ensure skill-task alignment so it honors the skills of every team member. This is also reflected in how we approach team leadership. We are more focused on leadership competencies as opposed to the leaders' subject matter expertise. A leader can learn new subject matter but must have leadership competencies to lead the team.

Lynne Chafetz

If someone from the outside were to come into a meeting of the executive team it would be hard to know who was in clinical work and who was in business practices. Our leadership team understands how to use this methodology to create reliable care across the continuum. I look forward to the day when people do not say, "Do you train doctors by themselves? Or nurses?" That question implies a lack of understanding of how the work is really done.

Diane Miller

Our focus on respectful behaviors has equalized teams throughout the organization. I take great hope for the future of medicine in knowing that in our Graduate Medical Education programs residents and fellows at Virginia Mason learn not only to be doctors but also to be effective team members. This takes patient safety to a whole new level.

Kathleen Paul

I think about my last trip to Japan: we had nurses, we had doctors, we had front desk people, people from KPO, and we were all working on the same project. There was *no* hierarchy, and sometimes the best ideas came from people who weren't in any way involved in leadership. Another example is the mandatory flu shot where a medical assistant came up with the idea and the whole organization followed. I suspect that that doesn't happen in very many organizations.

Dr. Joyce Lammert

Having worked in other organizations—I think a fundamental difference is the trust and collaboration among administrators and physician leaders. We are all striving for the same thing and have important and recognized roles.

Cathie Furman

Our work is too complex to be delivered by lone helmsmen, special craftsmen, and idiosyncratic operators. The history of production is clear. Standardization and standard work reduce defects and costs. A well-defined job makes sense and breeds the creativity we need to find the next version of this job. Only multiskilled, cross-trained operators can align their various skills and deliver defect-free care.

Dr. Kim Pittenger

Courage

Charleen Tachibana does not mince words. When you ask her a question, you get a sharp, direct answer. When I asked her about the essential elements and she mentioned courage, I asked what she meant by that. "Courage to do things others are not doing," she promptly replied. "Courage to face the reality of our flaws and defects. Courage and vulnerability to make them transparent and talk about it."

We have the courage to be inspired by idea of zero defects and courage to look at things the way they really are and understand the current state. And we have the courage to try things and learn from failure and the courage to use a method that allows the people who know the work best to be truly heard and contribute to improving work in a way they others might not be able to.

Dr. Donna Smith

Creating an environment where people are willing to be honest about what is really going on in the organization requires that the leader's role model being open and honest. That takes a lot of courage.

Sarah Patterson

We have taken an unconventional path, we have listened to countless hours of skepticism and complaint, and we have felt lonely and isolated in our vision. But I think it is better to say that courage is something we received. We received it from our patients. By knowing the important things for our patients—safe care, appropriate care, quality care, efficient care—and by taking inspiration from the importance of these things, our patients gave us the courage to embark on this journey.

Dr. Bob Caplan

We're trying to build courage to be honest and supportive and share unvarnished truth when we have it and still maintain trust and collegiality. We have the courage to share unvarnished truth with patients and families.

Darlene Corkrum

I think it takes true courage to be a leader in the health care industry. Practicing true evidenced based medicine that chooses the economically less rewarding outcome or developing a culture that mandates being transparent with less than optimal outcomes are examples of the courage that is demonstrated by our organization. And one of the reasons I am so proud to work here.

Dr. Catherine Potts

It was not insignificant when we as a leadership group chose to look outside for another way to produce health care. No other organization was doing that in any significant way and for our team to choose to adopt a manufacturing methodology took a lot of courage. There were many naysayers both within and external to the organization.

Cathie Furman

We have the courage to take the long view. The death of Mrs. McClinton and our willingness to do the right thing and talk about that very publicly with the aim to ensure that would not happen somewhere else. That took courage. And we have the courage to listen every day to what the staff is saying and not be defensive when we hear what is not going right.

Lynne Chafetz

One of the things about innovation and creativity is that you are doing something you have never done before. Vulnerability as a leader is directly linked to courage, which is linked to innovation. We are trying to create a courageous culture where ideas and vulnerability are rewarded.

Steve Schaefer

Transparency

As noted already, Tachibana does not mince or waste words. When I asked her about the role of transparency in Virginia Mason's improvement efforts she replied, "If you can't see it you can't improve it."

Transparency connects to vulnerability of leaders—here is what we are up against and how we need to work together as a team; the respect we show the front line by being transparent.

Diane Miller

When something goes wrong, we work to understand what exactly it was that went wrong and we inform patients. Without having transparent conversations we can't improve.

Lynne Chafetz

The commitment to transparency for me is also about the ability to face my physicians in an area that I'm responsible for and say, "I absolutely agree. We are not meeting your needs. We're not meeting the flows. We're not doing what is expected of us and here's why. Here's what we know. Here's what we plan to do." And being completely open about that and asking for help. Being open and vulnerable to say, "I don't have all the answers. This is what we think we're going to do about it. What do you think?" Visibility is the key to revealing waste and defects. One of the proudest moments we ever had was the transparency around the loss of Mary McClinton.

Steve Schaefer

Transparency is a state of mind. So many in other organizations fear the implications, but what we have found is being transparent about a mistake actually can add value and meaning to the work.

Cathie Furman

Performance transparency reveals the current state, generates tension for change, and aligns the group. System dysfunction causes variation. There is no shame in having lower performance as long as we submit to kaizen methods and team up to change the current state. We have no right to be privately random.

Dr. Kim Pittenger

We have a firm belief that information and processes are transparent to everyone. In the clinic, the metrics are available to the entire team. This improves trust and allows us to have the crucial conversation to make the necessary changes. In addition, quality and cost metrics are moving to full transparency for our patients.

Jim Cote

Alignment

One of the more unusual aspects about Virginia Mason—certainly compared with other health care organizations—is the alignment that helps define the leadership and the organizational culture. Patterson notes, "Having *all* of the executives accountable for *all* of the organizational goals has been one of the most important things we have done to create alignment. It insures that we are all aware of the progress of work that is being done and we are all motivated to remove any barriers. The work has our attention and that sends an important signal to the entire organization."

I can't even imagine how we would lead if we didn't have our Strategic Plan. How would everyone know what is most important to us? Although developing alignment can take time, once you have it, you can move at the speed of light.

Sue Anderson

Alignment is our daily fuel. Alignment with our vision, our goals, our leaders, and each other—that's what powers our daily work. That's the energy source for building great teams, keeping focused and accountable, maintaining urgency, and removing distraction and embracing new lessons.

Dr. Bob Caplan

The discipline of kaizen reaps results. Results recruit trust. People align when they trust the direction. Alignment yields reliability.

Dr. Kim Pittenger

In leadership we all speak the language of VMPS and that enables us to partner and collaborate together.

Steve Schaefer

Our success in aligning our entire medical center toward our shared purpose has been greatly facilitated by the widespread knowledge and use of our strategic pyramid. By graphically depicting our patient at the top, we remind everyone of our mission to improve the health and well- being of the patients we serve.

Dr. Catherine Potts

The obvious ultimate principle that aligns us is the patient. And with our management method if we have a moment of misalignment it is easy to get back in alignment because of our vision, strategy and processes. Visitors come here and frequently comment on how when they listen to us they can hear the alignment in what we talk about and how we talk about our work.

Diane Miller

I forget that clarity of alignment here is such a unique attribute until I go someplace else and see a lot less alignment and clarity. For us it's clearly all about making it better for patients. At other organizations you listen to all the other agendas around the room.

Dr. Donna Smith

One of many things we do to create alignment is produce a monthly line-up tool to help managers connect the dots for team members. This tool is a discussion starter that prompts us all to have the same conversation at the same time. Having team members around the organization focused on a single topic is remarkably powerful.

Kathleen Paul

Learning Organization

Steve Schaefer has an interesting take on one of the elements that distinguishes Virginia Mason: "We are a learning organization vs. a punitive organization. Our patient safety alert system is a major aspect of that as is Friday report-out where there are always lessons learned. Every time we do something we learn from it."

You have to understand that to create a learning organization, the leaders have to become teachers, coaches, and mentors and are no longer the ones who decide what needs to be improved and how we will improve it. I think you could describe that as learning to give up control in order to get control.

Sarah Patterson

Our being a learning organization manifests itself for the most part in the idea that failure is not something to be feared. We have the ability to say, "That didn't quite work, so what is the next PDSA (Plan, Do, Study, Act)?" Of all the things after 10-plus years I'm most proud of, it's that we are a learning organization and our constant changing and improvement is a reflection of that learning.

Diane Miller

Willingness to understand what works and what does not work. The ability to be humble and realize you don't know it all and we need to continue to challenge ourselves to learn new ways. This is personal learning as well as organizational learning. The more we know, the more we realize we don't know.

Charleen Tachibana

I can't imagine working in an organization that isn't constantly learning and improving. In a learning organization we are motivated by our learning and the improvements they yield. It instills a sense of pride in all who work here.

Sue Anderson

We took one of the darkest moments in our history, the preventable death of Mrs. Mary McClinton, and made it the rallying cry to inspire team members to focus on the safety of each patient. By embracing this tragedy, we made it a catalytic event for the organization.

Kathleen Paul

Our strategic pillar around innovation is very important along with VMPS as we seek to train every member of the team to speak up and understand where improvement is needed. We try things, and there are times when we celebrate failure. Every Friday report-out part of standard work is reporting on lessons learned.

Lynne Chafetz

By what methods are we going to improve quality? What are the operating principles and rudiments of these methods? How do we make sure we all learn the rudiments? We must build a system for learning. We must commit to teaching in flow at every teachable moment once we are trained.

Dr. Kim Pittenger

We are continually looking for new ideas and new ways to do things. Learning is an important part of who we are. It's a complete learning organization where we share our learning from an improvement event with other areas of the organization and spread this work. There is a core belief that we can always learn and do better.

Jim Cote

Accountability

Accountability is one of the most frequently heard words from leaders at Virginia Mason, for it serves as a kind of fuel that helps propel the VMPS management system. Patterson talks about building accountability into any new process. "We need to identify the feedback loops—how will the team members in this process know if they aren't following it correctly? And we need to identify the metrics we will use to measure the performance of the process on an ongoing basis and make it visible to all team members."

My accountability as a leader is holding people accountable for what we say so that behaviors match our words. I can't feel uncomfortable when I hold someone accountable for his or her performance. Health care is riddled with people not holding each other accountable because we might feel bad.

Diane Miller

Built into systems are processes that make things visible and hold us all accountable. This is really a critical leadership function. Early in our VMPS journey there were a number of people waiting to see if that was going to go away. We held to our vision and made it very transparent.

Lynne Chafetz

Leadership is usually vertical, but we are creating more accountability along horizontal value streams. Boeing is an example. Historically, people were accountable for components of the plane, but in today's world at Boeing they are accountable for the 737.

Steve Schaefer

When the work is standard and visible—it is much easier to see any defects and therefore make sure it is corrected. Standard Work for Leaders huddle boards have helped tremendously not only hold the leader accountable but also engage the staff who can see what is being worked on and how they can help with their ideas for improvement.

Cathie Furman

When I think about accountability and reflect on our journey, I can see great moments from the leaders and areas of opportunity. Two examples stand out: (1) when something goes wrong, the leader "protects" the employee and focuses on the system; and (2) when the leader consistently promotes or acknowledges their direct reports who have stayed true to our values, our vision, and our management method.

Linda Hebish

I feel acutely accountable for what I contribute to the whole. If I don't deliver, I let the entire team down.

Sue Anderson

Urgency

Discussing urgency in the context of health care is a tricky business. While there is a sense of urgency for improvement at Virginia Mason it doesn't have the full intensity that Kaplan or any of the other members of the leadership team would like to see. Why? In part because sustaining a sense of urgency is a challenge in any business. "If you don't have urgency none of the transformative changes we must make will happen," says Kaplan. Diane Miller puts it this way: "Leaders in health care do not have enough urgency. On an aircraft carrier they do it perfectly every time. That is urgency—to do it perfectly every time. In health care, patients are harmed all the time, and we still don't seem to have that urgency."

> We are frequently having conversations as leaders about how we could be much more effective as an organization. It is just a regular part of our day to question what could be improved. We know we could be so much better. Questioning is very important to creating urgency on an ongoing basis.
>
> **Sarah Patterson**

> We have no time to waste. We are talking about people being injured and dying in our care that should not be dying. The longer we take the more people are being harmed.
>
> **Charleen Tachibana**

> A shared sense of urgency is one of the key drivers that pushes all of us to try to continually do better. Everyone understands that making our processes safer, eliminating waste, and reducing costs are all things that cannot wait until tomorrow if we are going to be successful in being the quality leader today.
>
> **Dr. Catherine Potts**

> Fail forward fast, using structured empirical methods. We are not operating in the terrain of randomized controlled trials. Pick a method and use it. There is no constant but change.
>
> **Dr. Kim Pittenger**

Urgency is embedded in our production system. It is easy in health care to be complacent. The status quo is a black hole. We try and create a vision for our teams that we have no time and have to change today for the sake of our patients and staff.

Lynne Chafetz

Leaders must maintain a sense of urgency, or status quo will set in. At Virginia Mason, leaders revisit this in routine settings—at Tuesday standup. Gary may remark on a recent improvement and then remind us that we haven't reached 100% quality. Or the leader on point for Friday report-outs will review the tremendous amount of work accomplished, acknowledging the hard work, and subtly remind us that there is more work to be done. What we've just witnessed may have improved 15 areas, but there are 150 more areas where the same improvement may apply.

Linda Hebish

The more we do and the more we improve the greater the urgency. As we move forward we understand how much further we have to go. The sense of getting to zero defects creates urgency that each of us internalizes. Otherwise, we are harming our patients. The most important type of urgency—the type that leads to major improvements—is the urgency that comes from within as you feel the need to get better for our patients and our staff.

Sue Anderson

The essential elements—the foundational characteristics and attributes upon which Virginia Mason's success has been—are powerful in and of themselves. Focusing on the role that courage plays in the Virginia Mason story, for example, reveals a great deal about the leadership, culture, and the missionary zeal with which the team pursues the perfect patient experience. The same holds true for the other essential elements—for optimism, humility, alignment, accountability, learning organization, courage, urgency, teamwork, and transparency.

But I think at the end of the day when considering these various elements they seem to me not so much a collection of individual characteristics but connected elements of something larger. I think of the individual elements as woven together so that each strand is part of the whole. Woven together, these strands form a beautiful and highly practical seamless garment—a garment that derives its strength, warmth, and healing powers from the synergistic relationship among all of the woven strands. It is this garment that protects, soothes, heals, and guides Virginia Mason patients and the team of men and women who serve those patients.

Endnotes

The vast majority of the material for this book came during scores of interviews with a wide variety of clinicians and administrators at Virginia Mason. Prior to writing this book I had accumulated a good deal of knowledge about Virginia Mason based on earlier writing I had done about the work there. This included a chapter about Virginia Mason in my book *The Best Practice: How the New Quality Movement Is Transforming Medicine*, PublicAffairs (2008). My prior work also included the book *Transforming Healthcare: Virginia Mason Medical Center's Pursuit of the Perfect Patient Experience*, CRC Press (November 8, 2010). Serving as editor of the Virginia Mason blog for two years added depth to my understanding of the work.

Chapter One

I relied upon the article "A Production System for Health Care: At Virginia Mason Standard Processes Cut Waste, Improve Quality" by Todd Sloane, Press Ganey Partners, Issue 25, Sept/Oct. 2012.

http://www.slideshare.net/BradKruger/sep-oct-2012-partners-pressganey

Chapter Four

"Medical Disrespect: Bullying doctors are not just unpleasant they are dangerous. Can we change the culture of intimidation in our hospitals?" by Ilana Yurkiewicz appeared in Aeon Magazine, January 29, 2014; http://aeon.co/magazine/health/why-rude-doctors-make-bad-doctors/

The work of Bob Emiliani was a rich source for this chapter, particularly his book *Real Lean: The Keys to Sustaining Lean Management (Volume Three)*, The Center for Lean Business Management, LLC, (May 12, 2008). I relied in particular on Appendix I from that book, "The Equally Important 'Respect for People' Principle." It was through Emiliani's work in this Appendix that I learned of and relied upon: *Toyota Production System: Beyond Large-Scale Production* by Taiichi Ohno; Portland, Oregon: Productivity Press, 1988; and a memo entitled "Corporate Culture: Toyota's Secret, Competitive Advantage" by Michael Husar, 1991.

Chapter Seven

I relied upon the article "Put It in Writing: Virginia Mason's board compact drives accountability and performance," by Jamie Orlikoff and Gary Kaplan in the journal *Trustee*, Sept. 2012.

http://www.trusteemag.com/display/TRU-news-article.dhtml?dcrPath=/templatedata/HF_Common/NewsArticle/data/TRU/Magazine/2012/Sep/1209TRU_FEA_Writing

Chapter Eight

I relied upon interviews with leaders from the North Shore Physicians Group as well as North Shore Medical Center including Bob Norton, Steve Kapfhammer, Drs. Maury McGough, Craig Grimes, and Mitch Rein. From Summit Health I relied upon Niki Showe, Pat O'Donnell, Drs. Frank Mozdy and Kevin Lorentsen, as well as Bea Hoffman, and James Pryor. At the Virginia Mason Institute I relied upon Diane Miller, Dr. Henry Otero, and Chris Backous.

Index

Printed in the United States
by Baker & Taylor Publisher Services